After the show Kenzie was about to go off in search of a Coke when she heard a familiar shriek. "Hi, Billy! I just wanted to tell you that I love your new CD! I think it's the best one you've ever done. I play it all the time!"

Kenzie could only stare. The Christian music star smiled kindly. Emily beamed, then practically screamed the words Kenzie had imagined only in her worst nightmare:

"Billy, my suitemate is from Nashville! Could I get an extra autograph for her? She's not here, she had to go someplace with her dad. Her name's Kenzie Dawson—"

Kenzie plastered herself against the concrete wall near the side of the stage and waited breathlessly for Billy's response.

Billy looked at Emily in confusion. "What do you mean? Kenzie and her dad were here just before the show. Where'd they go?"

NUMBER 3

TRUE IDENTITY

BY BERNIE SHEAHAN

TRUE IDENTITY
published by Palisades
a part of the Questar publishing family

© 1996 by Bernie Sheahan
International Standard Book Number: 0-88070-949-9

Cover photography by Mike Houska
Cover designed by Kevin Keller

Printed in the United States of America.

To Jill E. Freeman,
my inordinately gifted fellow writer
and honorary co-author,

with love, laughter and deep gratitude to God,
Barry Hannah, and the University of Mississippi writing program
for our extraordinary friendship—
a most joyful surprise during the writing of this book.
"Gee whiz!," she exclaimed dorkily.

To the "Kenzies" in my life, my inspirations for this story:
Courtney A. Coker, Kendall J. Hooker Hinote,
Mackenzie Anne Mader, Emily Mackenzie Hall, Kristin Smith,
my friends in the "fishbowl" (and their kids),
and all the Young Life "kids" I've ever loved.

To those faithful RELEASE, Aspire and CCM readers.

…and to my family—especially Mom,
my first and best English teacher.

May we find our true identity as the kids
of our very rich, influential and loving Father.

ALL I EVER HAVE TO BE

When the weight of all my dreams
Is resting heavy on my head
and the thoughtful words of help and hope
Have all been nicely said
But I'm still hurting, wondering if I'll ever be the one
I think I am—I think I am.

Then You gently re-remind me
That You've made me from the first
And the more I try to be the best
The more I get the worst
And I realize the good in me.

And all I ever have to be is what You've made me
Any more or less would be a step out of Your plan
As you daily recreate me help me always keep in mind
That I only have to be what I can find
And all I ever have to be
All I have to be
All I ever have to be is what You've made me.

GARY CHAPMAN
1979 PARAGON MUSIC CORP.

Special thanks to the staff of Riverstone Airlines.

1

Why didn't I eat before I got on the plane? These are totally science-project eggs. A *C-minus* project." Kenzie Dawson stared at the plastic tray in front of her, dimpled cheeks folding into a grimace.

"I do this every time I have to take an early flight, and then I'm sorry. Did your mom make you eat this morning, Ethan?"

From his seat across the aisle, Ethan Brooks nodded amiably, his mouth full of his own "science-project" airline omelet. Washing it down with orange juice from a carton, he gulped and turned to Kenzie.

"Yeah...we drove through Mickey D's on the way to your house. Had an Egg McMuffin and a couple of milks. And then those blueberry muffins your mom made for me and my folks. Man, those were good. Plus, my mom made up a bunch of ham-and-biscuits for the trip. Want some?"

Kenzie looked at Ethan, all 135 pounds of him, lean and wiry in his flannel shirt and jeans. "How on earth can you put away so much food and still be so skinny?"

Ethan was quick at the draw. "You're one to talk. You're the first girl I've ever met who could suck down a large milkshake and then eat a fudge bar on top of it. How come *you* never gain any weight?"

His teasing was par for the course in their relationship, and Kenzie relished every minute of it. Usually shy and reserved, Ethan could be uncharacteristically chatty in her presence.

As the only two Tennesseans at Seattle's Pacific Cascades University, Kenzie and Ethan shared a special bond. During the previous summer, Ethan had taken the suggestion of a woman from the registrar's office and had written Kenzie a letter, introducing himself. Soon afterward, the two families met at Ethan's home, near the Dawsons' summer vacation cabin in the Great Smoky Mountains of East Tennessee. The friendship between PCU's two incoming freshmen was nearly instantaneous, and the bond had been strengthened in the fall when Kenzie's parents invited Ethan to join them and Kenzie in driving cross-country to school. In the months since, Ethan became the brother Kenzie—as the youngest of four girls—had never had.

"I *have* gained weight, Brooks!" Kenzie retorted, in response to Ethan's question about her eating habits. "I'm working on the freshman fifteen! Haven't you noticed? Oh, I forgot—you don't notice that sort of thing on me; I'm like your sister. Besides, you're too busy checkin' out my suite-mates, huh? Like Emily, maybe?"

"Whatever…" Ethan shrugged, but turned red in the face.

Kenzie relented. "I'm kidding. I'll probably never get fat. It's a metabolism thing, you understand. But you're right about the ice cream addiction. It's not one I plan to get over."

In between comments to Ethan, Kenzie had managed to polish off the same omelet she'd held in disdain just moments earlier.

"So where're these ham-and-biscuits you're talking about,

huh? I'm still hungry." Kenzie grinned, making her dimples disappear almost completely into her impish face. This morning, as on many mornings, her chestnut-colored hair was pulled back in a ponytail and tucked under a Seattle Mariners baseball cap, which highlighted her sleep-deprived, but laughing, blue eyes.

"I'll get 'em." Ethan fumbled in his carry-on bag and pulled out a large, plastic Ziplock bag. "Here. Country ham and homemade biscuits, courtesy of Andrea Brooks."

Kenzie took one of the treats and sniffed it admiringly.

"I don't get it, E," said Kenzie. "Your mom isn't even from the South, and she makes these killer biscuits. Isn't she from Ohio or somewhere? What's wrong with this picture? Not that I'm complaining." She popped the small biscuit and slice of salty ham in her mouth, whole, and raised her eyebrows in delight.

"You should know, Kenzie; if you live in the Smoky Mountains, you have to make ham-and-biscuits. It's a Tennessee state law," Ethan joked. "Actually, I think she learned it from one of the cooks at the park restaurant."

Kenzie raised her eyes at Ethan's reference to the Great Smoky Mountains National Park, where his dad was a ranger. Kenzie's family had roots close to the eastern Tennessee border of the park, and Kenzie had a thousand childhood memories of hiking in the Smokies, just a few miles from where her Scotch-Irish ancestors had long ago eked out a living as subsistence farmers. During summer weeks spent at the Dawsons' mountain cabin, she had grown to love the Smoky Mountains, with their thick forest of evergreen and hardwood trees. When it came time to think about a college major, Kenzie had picked forestry, more from a romanticized notion of life as a forest ranger than an affinity for science. Consequently, she was curious about every aspect of Ethan's life at the park.

"The park restaurant? They have the *best* catfish I've ever eaten in my life. I'm not kidding. Did they teach your mom how to fry it?"

"Nope," said Ethan. "She's adapted to Southern cooking pretty well, but she hates catfish. Sometimes Dad and I go down to the park restaurant when we get a craving. You know, I wish they had catfish at the PCU cafeteria."

"Yeah, right!" Kenzie let out a gut laugh at the thought of PCU's too-cool West Coast kids eating fried catfish and "hush puppies," the deep-fried, oniony dough balls that only a Southerner could love. "You know what, Ethan? That's making me hungry. Would you hand me another biscuit, please?"

"Geez, Kenzie. Maybe you should go easy on it. Didn't you tell me you've barfed on a plane before?"

"Well, yeah…but only a couple of times." Kenzie thought for a moment. "Okay, ten. But I travel a lot, so that's not too bad, considering. And it's only when the turbulence is really rough, or I haven't had enough sleep, or —"

"So when did you go to bed last night, anyway?" Ethan looked at her skeptically, as if evaluating his chances at being called upon to play nursemaid.

"Ummm, I don't know. Four? I was packing, and my sisters and I were talking—"

"And you had to get up about two hours later, didn't you? Great. And now you've had a science-project omelet and two ham biscuits. That makes me nervous." Ethan *did* look nervous.

Kenzie rushed to reassure him. "I'm not going to hurl, Ethan! I'm fine, really. I just need to take a little nap. Are you gonna use that pillow?"

As the flight attendant picked up the remains of their much-maligned breakfast, Kenzie flipped her tray table up and pushed the button to recline the seat.

"Hey, look at this, E. In all my years of flying, this has always cracked me up: Look how far back the seat goes. A whole two inches! Like that's a big deal."

Kenzie demonstrated, to Ethan's amusement, the two-inch difference between uprightness and recline. "Up, down. Forward, back. Torture, bliss. Misery, perfection. Great, isn't it?"

The snappily dressed businesswoman seated directly behind Kenzie cleared her throat, obviously annoyed.

"I'm so sorry! I didn't realize you were back there." Kenzie craned her neck to flash the Dawson smile. After chatting pleasantly with the woman for a good three minutes, she turned back to Ethan.

He looked at her in amazement. "You're unbelievable, Kenzie. You can talk to anyone, can't you?" He watched as she continued to play with the buttons on her seat's armrest. "I never really noticed about the seat thing. You gotta remember that my family doesn't travel like yours does. We've never been to Africa or the Grand Caymans, or anything like that."

"What's that supposed to mean?" Kenzie said, feeling vaguely hurt.

"Nothin'." Ethan's voice held no trace of envy. "Just that your life is so different from mine, that's all. I never would have noticed these little irritations on the plane. I hardly ever fly; I think it's cool."

"That's why you're sitting by the window," Kenzie nodded. "Sure sign of a rookie traveler. Aisle seats give you so much more freedom." She stopped short, realizing how she sounded. "Sorry. I didn't mean anything by it."

"Neither did I, Kenzie…I just think it's cool that your family gets to do all that stuff, that's all. And that you're not stuck up about being rich."

13

Kenzie pulled off her Mariners cap, smoothed her hair, and clapped the cap back on her head. "I just hate talking about it, that's all. I can't help it if my parents have made some money."

"*Some* money?" Ethan laughed. "They just own LightSong Records, the biggest Christian record company in Nashville—the world, for Pete's sake. By the way...are you ever going to tell anyone at school about it?

Kenzie turned toward him and frowned. "It *is* starting to get to me, E. It's just that I want to see what life is like without being known as 'Johnny Dawson's daughter.' I just want to be *me*. I want people to like me for who I am, not because I know famous music people."

"But you love your family, and you love those friends—" Ethan broke off his argument. "I guess I understand, though. I just wonder how long you'll get away with your generic 'my dad's a corporate executive.'"

"My suite-mates *are* starting to get suspicious," Kenzie sighed. "Emily keeps catching me with those packages from our company—Dad's assistant sends me every new CD before it's in the stores. Emily thinks they're from J. Crew or something, thank goodness. I mean, Em is the biggest Christian music freak in the whole school. If she knew about my family, she'd never leave me alone!"

Ethan reclined his seat the full two inches. "I know. When I help her with her Christian radio show at the campus station, she about drives me nuts in between songs, talking about all those artists." From anyone else, the words would have sounded like a criticism, but Ethan's fondness for Emily showed in his gentle tone. "No offense, but I'm just not that into Christian music."

Kenzie laughed and leaned back on the pillow, deciding not to tease Ethan about his slight crush. "No problem, E. I have to be into it, though—it's putting me through college." She grinned at the look Ethan gave her. "I'm *kidding*…some of it's pretty great. Especially LightSong stuff, of course. My dad sent you some CDs, didn't he? He likes you. So does my mom. She's probably going to want me to marry you one day. Just warning you."

"Marry you? No way." Ethan managed a shy grin. "I know you too well. Your parents are cool, though." He paused. "I'd consider marrying your sister, after meeting your family at the cabin last summer."

"Which one? I've got two single ones, you know."

"Leighton. She's a total babe."

"Elizabeth Leighton Dawson the Fourth? She's five years older than you! She'd drive you crazy. Besides, she's a neat freak."

"And you're not?"

"I'm *not* a neat freak. I have a place for everything, that's all. Not like my slob suite-mates, bless their hearts."

"Cooper, you mean. Well, she's got all that weirdo New York stuff to mess with."

"Can you believe her? And Beth, the Phantom. She's always with her boyfriend, but she somehow manages to mess up our room in the five minutes she's there. Drives me crazy."

"Do they know about your dirty little secret: that your dad played guitar with Elvis, then discovered Billy Weber, the Christian pop star, and made a fortune with LightSong Records?"

"Nope. Beth could care less. Cooper might be interested, but Emily…whoa. I can't bear to think of what life would be like if she knew. She'd be begging me to tell her what Billy Weber eats for breakfast."

"Oh, give her a break." Ethan looked at Kenzie slyly. "But,

now that you mention it, what *does* he eat?"

Kenzie took it in stride. "He eats anything. Cereal-wise, if you must know, he and Susan both love Grape-Nuts. Not me. It's like eating gravel—you chew, and chew, and chew. How do you know when to swallow?"

Ethan shook his head with a wry smile. "You are so weird. Okay, so who else knows about your family, besides me? Alicia Raju? Allie must know; she's your new best friend at school. Besides me, of course."

"Allie..." Kenzie shook her head. "I can't believe it took us till November to run into each other at PCU. We had such a blast at camp two years ago, but did she write and tell me she was going to PCU? Nooooo. I had to run into her in the library, of all places."

"I'm glad y'all hooked up again. She's cool." Ethan nodded approvingly.

A wide smile spread across Kenzie's face. "I can't wait to see her! She said she'd pick us up at the airport. Who knows what she'll have waiting for us!"

"There's no telling," said Ethan with a look of mock dread. "Allie is the only girl on campus who is weirder than you."

"Thanks a lot," Kenzie said cheerfully, taking his comment as a compliment. "Remember when she picked us up after Thanksgiving? Wasn't that great? Holding up that huge sign at the gate: 'Mr. and Mrs. Nude Tennessee'—I thought I was gonna die!"

"You handled it pretty well. But, man, I was never so embarrassed in my life!"

"Aww, c'mon. You know you loved it, E. You've led a sheltered life, out there in the woods. You needed a little loosening up, Mr. Home School."

"Hey!" Ethan rose to defend himself. "I liked home schooling. It gave me a lot of freedom that I wouldn't have had in a regular school."

"Green Hills Academy wasn't exactly 'regular,' either," said Kenzie. "All of those rich preppy white kids, exactly the same, getting BMWs and Range Rovers for their 16th birthdays."

"And we don't have our share of those at PCU?"

"Yeah, but at least everyone's not *exactly* the same. It's fun to have friends that aren't all Baptist or Presbyterian. Names like Yamashiro and Contarini and Raju—kids from cool places like Vancouver and California. Like Allie. Remember, I told you we met two summers ago at Malibu, the Young Life camp? I remember, I thought she was so cool. Her parents came here from India, you know."

"The West Coast is really different from good ol' Tennessee," Ethan agreed. "But at least you have coffeehouses in Nashville. We're not quite that hip in Sevier County."

"I did get to hang at Bongo Java over Christmas break. It was so cool. All those public school kids with weird hair and nose rings. It's just as cool as The Cup and Chaucer. Let's get a bunch of us and go to The Cup tonight, okay? Buy you a latté."

"Sure," Ethan said amiably. "How handy for you that Chris Gallagher is probably playing there tonight. If you drool on the table again, I'm walking out," he teased.

"Whatever." Kenzie forced herself to sound casual. "There was no actual drool. I just think he's really good on guitar, that's all."

"Uh-huh." Ethan looked unconvinced. "So when are you going to admit that you have a crush on him, and give him a big career break by introducing him to your dad?"

Kenzie groaned and twisted in her seat, trying to get comfortable. "I don't want to think about it now, E. I'm tired."

Ethan didn't say another word. Grabbing another ham biscuit from the bag, he clamped on his Walkman headphones and left Kenzie to her thoughts.

Too wired to sleep, Kenzie stuck in tiny foam earplugs, hoping that the muted sounds and the vibration of the plane would lull her into dreamland. Despite her efforts, however, her thoughts continued to dart between Nashville and Seattle—from the three weeks of comfortable familiarity of home to the uncertainties of the spring semester ahead at PCU. From the old friends and beloved family in Tennessee to her new friends at school.

Like Chris Gallagher. Kenzie had seen him at orientation in September and remembered meeting him during her fabulous week at the Young Life resort in British Columbia. Kenzie's Malibu experience had introduced her to so many things—great new friends from the West Coast, parasailing, the appeal of her Southern accent (which Kenzie always used to her advantage while charming the West Coast boys), and a renewed sense of excitement about her relationship with God.

Eight hours by boat from Vancouver up the Princess Louisa Inlet, Malibu was an old yachting resort, bought on a prayer and a vision by Young Life's founder in the 1950s. His motto "It's a sin to bore a kid with the gospel" was lived out at Malibu, where Young Life's outrageously fun, adventuresome outreach to teenagers invited kids to consider the claims of Christ in a non-threatening environment, surrounded by some of the most beautiful scenery in the world.

Though Kenzie had grown up in a committed Christian home, she'd had a superficial relationship with God until she'd gone to a Young Life club at Green Hills Academy. During her week at Malibu, she'd confronted issues of faith and come to understand God's grace in a new way. She'd also started thinking about going to PCU, since quite a few of the kids at camp were planning to enroll.

Including Chris Gallagher, the quiet boy with the winning smile and the permanently attached guitar. When other kids were parasailing and waterskiing, Chris was perched on a rock, overlooking the inlet, lost in a musical world of his own.

She remembered seeing him again at PCU's orientation, and how it had suddenly occurred to her where they'd met.

"Chris?" she'd asked, squinting to read his name tag on that bright September afternoon. "You went to Young Life camp at Malibu, two summers ago, right? You're the guitar guy—oh, I'm Kenzie, by the way. Kenzie Dawson."

It had seemed obvious at the time that Chris remembered her quite well.

"Kenzie…" he'd said, rather dreamily, as she remembered it. "How could I forget that name? I think we were square dance partners or something. I remember your accent, mostly."

The memory of Chris—standing in the quad with his summer-blond hair cut blunt and parted in the middle, his inquisitive eyes and his honest, kind face searching Kenzie's own—was set in Kenzie's mind like the familiar pearl inlays on her guitar.

"Aren't you from the South somewhere?" he'd asked.

"Tennessee. Nashville, actually." Kenzie had wanted to tell him, right then and there, that she loved music as much as he did, that she understood his reveries with his guitar, on the rock, at Malibu.

But she didn't tell him anything of the sort, even when he'd expressed an interest in Nashville.

"Gruhn Guitars! Great vintage instruments. I have their catalog. Wow, I'd love to go there and just look."

She was dying to tell him that she'd been there, many times, when Dad indulged his penchant for buying fine, old guitars. She wondered if Chris would be impressed by the fact that she'd met Bob Dylan, Paul McCartney, and other music legends who frequented Gruhn's. The thought alarmed her, as she didn't want him to like her because of the celebrities she'd known.

"Yeah, I know what you mean." That was all Kenzie had volunteered. She'd longed to tell him that she knew exactly how it felt to get lost in the music. But she'd fudged it a little, telling Chris only, "I played guitar some in high school."

It wasn't really a lie, she recalled, as she shifted in her airplane seat. Although all four of the Dawson sisters loved music, Kenzie was clearly the one who'd inherited her father's extraordinary gift. But she also had other things to do, like play point guard for the GHA Lady Rebels basketball team, hike the Radnor Lake trails, cruise the streets of Nashville with a Jeepload of friends—the usual high school stuff.

It was true that Kenzie's dad and her Uncle Floyd had appeared on the Grand Ole Opry as The Little Dawson Brothers, at ages 11 and 12. After that, in the Sixties, Johnny Dawson's astounding proficiency on guitar had earned him a spot in Elvis's band. He'd become a "hot" country producer in Nashville, then almost single-handedly birthed Nashville's contemporary Christian music business in the Seventies and Eighties by discovering Billy Weber and founding LightSong Records. But he'd never forced or manipulated Kenzie into following his path, even though she was gifted. And she loved him for it.

Keeping her eyes closed, Kenzie rolled her head and languished over thoughts about her out-of-the-ordinary family and her covert attempts to distance herself from Nashville. Anonymity had been her motivation for choosing PCU over the University of Tennessee, which in actuality, had a much better forestry department.

At PCU, she could just be Kenzie Dawson. Not "personal friend of Billy Weber" or "Johnny Dawson's youngest," or even a pretty mean guitar picker. She could just be Kenzie. That's all. Mary Mackenzie Dawson, according to her birth certificate, her Tennessee driver's license and the admissions office at PCU, much to her chagrin. On the first day of class, professors always asked for "Mary," to which she was forced to respond, "It's Mary Mackenzie—please call me Kenzie." Consequently, more than one PCU student enjoyed calling her "Mac" or, worse, "Mary," which were fighting words, as far as she was concerned.

Chris Gallagher can call me anything he wants to…

Roused by that thought, Kenzie sat up rather suddenly, waking a half-asleep Ethan, who pulled his headphones off to hear what he was missing. "What? What is it?"

"Nothing. I just thought of something. Go back to sleep. I'm sorry."

Kenzie curled up again, brow furrowed, and thought about Chris. She had been fighting this crush with all her might, in an attempt to abide by her own Life Rule #1: Never Date a Musician—They're Flakes, Except for Dad.

The situation was further complicated by the fact that Chris was truly one of the most talented musicians she'd ever met outside of Nashville. Possibly the "next Billy Weber." In keeping both the secret of her attraction and the secret of her family's position, she was denying herself a possible relationship *and* keeping Chris from a potential shot at the "Big Time" in Nashville.

Kenzie glanced over at her friend. "Ethan? Since you're awake…are you up for talking?"

"Sure." Ethan sat up and yawned.

"It's just stuff that's been bothering me, and since you and Allie are the only ones that know about…well…" She looked at

Ethan for some sign of reassurance.

"I'm all ears."

Kenzie drew a deep breath. "I've been thinking...I've got to get my head together this semester, Ethan. I'm getting sort of tired of pretending to be somebody I'm not. Or maybe actually being who I am for a change. But I hate to lie about it." Kenzie realized she sounded as confused as she felt. "I mean...I'm not lying about it. I'm just not telling the truth. But that's just as bad as lying. Or is it? Maybe I should pray about this. Hey, what a concept!"

Ethan jerked Kenzie's sleeve, interrupting her monologue. "I'm sorry. The pilot's saying something, I think—"

The two strained to hear the pilot's calm report over the intercom, which informed passengers about upcoming turbulence over the Rockies.

Ethan looked worried. "Are you going to be okay, Kenzie? Did you take any airsickness pills or anything?"

Kenzie unfolded herself from the seat, stretched, yawned and pulled off her Mariners cap. "I forgot. But don't worry; I'll be okay. Will you? Does this scare you? The turbulence, I mean."

Kenzie, suddenly aware that Ethan was not a frequent flyer, tilted her head toward him with a concerned look. "Are you worried more about my possible hurling, or the bumpiness? It's nothing to worry about, I promise. It's just like potholes, but in the air. No big deal. We won't crash."

Ethan looked increasingly nervous. Just then, the plane hit an air pocket so hard it shook, and a few passengers gasped from fright.

"Dang! That was a good one!" Kenzie noticed, as did Ethan, that the Coke the flight attendant had brought him was sloshing furiously in the plastic cup.

"Okay, so we've got some potholes, just like bumps in the road, right?" said Kenzie, in an effort to calm Ethan's apparent fears and her own gurgling stomach. "Nothing to worry about, except for maybe potential puking...but I'm okay. Really, I am," she said, unconvincingly, thinking that Ethan needed comforting more than she did.

"Don't be scared of the bad air, E," Kenzie continued, trying to keep her mind off her own nausea. "You're a tough mountain man, remember? Davy Crockett wouldn't panic over a little turbulence, would he? Uh-oh..."

Kenzie felt tiny beads of sweat pop out on her forehead as the familiar feeling of nausea overcame her.

"Uh-oh. I think I should be worried about you," Ethan said nervously. As the narrow Super 80 plane trembled in the rough air, Kenzie felt sicker with every jolt.

"Are you okay, Kenzie?"

"Just talk to me, Ethan. Make me laugh. If I get my mind off it, I'll be okay. Really."

With hands shaking, Kenzie snapped her tray table down, yanked the ball cap from her head, and eased her damp face onto the cool plastic.

"Uh..." Ethan hesitated. "I'm not that funny...um...okay, how about this? Just think about The Cup and Chaucer tonight. You're going to see your friends, have a good time, drool over Chris..."

"Don't say drool! It's a bodily fluid...oh, gosh...E, I can't even think about latté, that makes me gag...get the flight attendant...I need some ginger ale..."

It was too late. In a quick, panicked move, Kenzie reached across Ethan to snatch the white paper airsickness bag from the seat pocket in front of him. Then, with a deft, if shaky, flourish, Kenzie pulled open the bag, leaned over, and let go.

Luckily for Ethan and the rest of the passengers, she was quiet about it. Leaning weakly against the seat, she set the bag on her tray table and folded the top, neatly crimping the wire stays to seal the contents safely inside.

"Oh, man. Ethan, get the flight attendant. I mean it. I need a ginger ale. This was major hurlage. I'm so embarrassed…"

Ethan pushed the button to summon the attendant, while looking at Kenzie with a mixture of horror and concern. "Are you gonna make it?"

"I'll be fine. As long as the rest of the ride is smooth. I feel so much better already, I swear. I probably shouldn't have gone for the second ham-and-b—oh. Ethan, promise me you won't tell anyone, not even your roommates. Okay? Promise? I'd be mortified."

"I promise," he answered quickly, then dashed down the narrow aisle in search of a flight attendant. Moments later, he returned with one. She was prepared for duty—bearing a cup of iced ginger ale and a cool, damp cloth, and wearing a sympathetic, motherly look. "You poor thing…here, let me take that," she said, picking up Kenzie's bag as casually if it were a sack from the deli.

"It won't be long now till we land, and the captain says it's smooth flying from here. Let me know if you need anything else, all right?"

"Thanks." Kenzie looked up at her like a sick puppy, grateful for a soothing pat on the head. Shakily, Kenzie took a long swig of ginger ale and held the cool cloth to her face. Within minutes, she was chatting with Ethan again, trying to forget what had just happened.

Before long, the plane dipped into its quick descent. As they began the long, slow turn around the Seattle-Tacoma area, the peaks of the Cascades and the Olympics came into view. The two peered out Ethan's window, admiring the stunning vista afforded by a rare clear day in Western Washington.

"Wow, check out Mount Rainier! Unbelievable! I can't wait to hike to the top one day," Kenzie exclaimed.

"You and me both," said Ethan. "Isn't it amazing, the difference between these mountains and our mountains? Our blue Smokies are so ancient and rounded, not spectacular like these."

"It's hard to say which you like better, isn't it? Guess it's like apples and oranges. This is stunning, and the Smokies are, well, they're great too. The Northwest is so…dramatic, but—"

"Yep, I know what you mean. I love Tennessee too, even if I wasn't born there."

"And here we are, in the great Pacific Northwest at last," said Kenzie, timing her announcement as the plane's wheels hit the runway and the brakes screeched to slow the aircraft's speed.

"Wonder what this semester's gonna be like?" Ethan mused, gathering his things. "So far, not so good. Starting off with major hurlage, I mean."

"E…you promised not to tell and I'm going to hold you to it!" Kenzie laughed, as she pointed her finger at her friend. They inched their way down the aisle, nodding to the flight crew on the way out. "We Tennesseans have to stick together, you know."

Halfway through the jetway, Kenzie and Ethan heard banjo music blaring from the gate area. They grinned at each other and said, knowingly, "—Allie!"

Kenzie gut-laughed and Ethan chuckled at the sight that met them: six of their PCU friends dressed in overalls and straw hats, with blacked-out teeth, carrying fake "moonshine" jugs. The entire group was singing loudly and off-key to a corny hillbilly song. Accompanying them was a real banjo player, who was picking fast and furiously. Allie Raju, the least authentic "hillbilly" of them all, grinned as she stomped her foot to the banjo and held up a sign that said, "WELCOME BACK, Y'ALL!" And behind the banjo player, Kenzie noticed, stood Chris Gallagher —wearing overalls, picking a lightning-fast guitar, and smiling at her.

Ethan, aware of Chris—and Kenzie's glance at him—smiled at Kenzie, too. "What was it you said? We Tennesseans have to stick together?"

Kenzie turned from Chris's gaze, scrunched her face into a dimpled grin, and winked at Ethan from under the bill of her Mariners cap. "You know, E, it's gonna be one heck of a semester. Ain't it?"

2

Kenzie dropped her bag with a thunk and ran toward the rowdy group. Ethan picked it up and followed her.

"Hey, y'all!" she yelled, running to hug everyone at the same time. "Look at y'all! You're incredible!"

"Hey, everybody." Ethan was typically subdued, compared to his boisterous fellow Tennessean.

While Chris and the banjo player kept the music going, Kenzie chatted with the rest of the group, which included Allie, her friend Drew, Kenzie's suite-mates Cooper and Emily, and Emily's brother, Ryan.

"We just wanted you to feel at home," said Allie, laughing. "Didn't want you to miss Tennessee or anything!"

Ever the practical joker, Allie had talked half-a-dozen of Kenzie's fellow freshmen into making complete fools of themselves at SEA-TAC, the busy Seattle-Tacoma International Airport. This was quite a feat, considering that Allie had only been a part of the gang since November. Even more impressive to Kenzie was the fact that Allie had secured the services of an honest-to-goodness banjo player, who, along with Chris on guitar, was doing a fine job ripping through a rapid-fire version of "Dueling Banjos." After the initial hilarity subsided, Kenzie gained her composure enough to get the details on her friend's latest prank.

"Allie! You dog! How in the world did you talk everybody into this? And where'd you get a real banjo player?"

"Easy!" said Allie, laughing. "I told 'em you're buying tonight at The Cup. The banjo player charges double, though. Two cappuccinos AND a biscotti."

"The Cup" Allie was referring to was The Cup and Chaucer, the same coffeehouse hangout Kenzie and Ethan had discussed on the plane. It was a cozy, bookish place, conveniently located near campus. With computers available at the side tables for customers to go "on-line," and informal, live entertainment in the evenings, The Cup was tremendously popular with PCU students.

Right now, Kenzie's favorite Cup and Chaucer entertainer stood not more than five feet away from her. As she chatted with Allie, Kenzie studied Chris out of the corner of her eye. He wore jeans ripped out at the knees with a rope belt to hold them around his slender waist, and his feet were bare, tapping out the rhythm of the old-timey tune. It was a good effort, but the look was more hippie than hillbilly—a fact Kenzie didn't mind one bit.

Allie gave Kenzie a playful nudge in the ribs as she noticed Kenzie's obvious stare. "I guess you noticed the surprise guest, huh? I ran into him this morning and he wanted to come. Yes, you owe me. Big time."

"Owe you?" Kenzie asked innocently. "I'm already buying for everybody, aren't I?" Kenzie said, swiftly changing the subject.

"Never mind! Hey, E!" Allie turned her attention toward Ethan, who was still holding his carry-on, laughing at the spectacle.

"Wow," was all he could muster, shaking his head in amazement at Allie's ingenuity.

Allie looked eagerly at Kenzie. "Did I get the vibe right, Kenz? Do you feel like you're still in the Smoky Mountains?"

"Close, Allie. Except that most Tennesseans are wearing shoes these days. The banjo was a nice touch, though, I'll admit. Who is this guy?"

"There was a notice on the bulletin board at the student union: 'Bluegrass Banjo Lessons', with a number. So I called, and he agreed to do it. Pretty impressive, huh?"

"Unbelievable. I still can't believe you got everybody to do it. Ryan, maybe. Drew, yeah. But Cooper? And Emily?"

"Like I said; I told 'em you were treating. You know my motto: FFTB, Free Food Tastes Better—or in this case, free cappuccino."

The hillbilly band gradually made its way to the baggage claim, where they continued to draw stares from other passengers. Chris Gallagher did an admirable job of keeping up with the bluegrass banjo player, and Allie continued to sing off-key, making up lyrics when she didn't know the song, which was most of the time. Kenzie, fully recovered from the Unfortunate Inflight Vomiting Incident, was in fine spirits, although she was struck with a sudden case of shyness in Chris Gallagher's presence.

"I'll go get the car, you guys. Keep it up!" Allie sprinted from the baggage claim toward the parking area. Kenzie and Ethan waited patiently for the baggage carousel to start.

"So, Kenzie, how was Christmas break? Tell me all about it!" Emily chirped.

On paper, Emily Stewart would have seemed like the kind of person Kenzie Dawson might have picked for a friend. Their rooms sported the same kind of feminine-tomboy touches, like solid colors, big plaid-print bedding, and baseball caps and favorite sweatshirts in the closets. Emily ran track in high school; Kenzie played basketball. But to Kenzie, Emily's goody-two-shoes attitude toward everything—school, friendships, faith—was a little grating. Emily played everything safe all the time, and to Kenzie, life just wasn't like that. Still, Em was more like Kenzie than Kenzie liked to admit. This made Kenzie feel even worse about the fact that she'd kept her suite-mate at arm's length, just because of the Christian music issue. *I'm going to try harder to be more friendly this semester,* she thought. *Starting now.*

"Hey, Em, what's up? Christmas was great, thanks. Nice outfit, by the way."

Emily's version of a hillbilly Tennessean was a cotton summer dress, under a denim jacket, with hiking boots and a cowboy hat. It was a great effort, Kenzie had to admit. On the wacky scale, though, it didn't hold a candle to Cooper's.

"COO-PER, where did you get that?"

Cooper Ellis, the token New Yorker in the circle of friends, wore a black fake-velvet jacket with an air-brushed picture of Elvis on the back. A waify looking thrift shop skirt and a clunky pair of black combat boots completed the outfit. Topping it off was a beat-up Minnie Pearl-style straw hat, complete with an obvious $1.29 price tag hanging from the brim.

"Had it all in my closet. Actually, I've worn all of this before, except for the Minnie Pearl hat, of course. Thrift shop, a dollar. Like it?"

"Yep, you win the prize. You got all the Tennessee elements. I'm not really sure about the combat boots, though." Kenzie smiled and glanced down at Cooper's feet.

Cooper scrunched up her face, thinking of a good answer. "Okay, how about the Tennessee National Guard?"

Minutes later, Allie burst through the automatic door, announcing that Kenzie's Jeep Cherokee was outside, on the curb.

"I'm illegally parked! Is your luggage here yet?"

"Allie, please don't get a ticket like you did after Thanksgiving. It's my car, you know!"

"Then I'd better go check on it…"

"That's okay; I will," volunteered Kenzie. "I missed my Cherokee when I was home." A thought occurred to her. "Hey, how were you planning to cram eight people and luggage in my car?"

"We can do it, Kenz! No problem. I'll drive, and you can sit on someone's lap." Allie gave Kenzie the "sly eye," in a not-so-subtle reference to Chris, who was still strumming away, enjoying this unusual jam session with the banjo player.

"Allie!" Kenzie whispered dramatically, while shooting her friend an "I'm going to kill you" look.

"Well, you know. I'm just trying to get this show on the road. If you don't go after him soon, I will. He is so *fine!"*

Kenzie rolled her eyes. Before she headed outside, she looked over at Chris and caught him watching her.

"Well, hey!" Chris abandoned the song to greet Kenzie. "What do you think? Could we play at the Grand Ole Opry?" He laughed—an easy, self-effacing laugh that endeared him to Kenzie even more. *He stopped in the middle of a song. Whoa…that's a big deal.*

"Sure! I'll call 'em for ya as soon as I get back to the dorm." *This is great…he has no idea that I actually know people there…*"Although I think you have a better future in rock and roll. With the outfit, I mean. They make people wear shoes at the Opry now."

He is so comfortable to be with. I can't believe I'm saying this.

31

Not that he'd ever suspect…

Chris grinned. "Did you have a good Christmas? Was Santa good to you? Oh—I'm sorry—have you gotten your bags yet? I can help you…"

Kenzie fairly melted at the gentlemanly overtures that seemed to come so naturally to him, flowing from the depth of his character, not some arbitrary societal niceties he'd been taught. She'd noticed that he was always considerate—with girls and guys, young or old. He was as respectful of the PCU cafeteria ladies as he was the senior professors. And though he was smart, articulate and unafraid to express his beliefs—which Kenzie had observed in their Philosophy 101 class fall semester—he wasn't argumentative or arrogant. *If Jesus came to PCU as a freshman, I bet he'd be a lot like Chris.*

"Yeah! Christmas was great! Oh, thanks, Chris…Ethan's getting the bags, I think. Um, excuse me…"

Kenzie was sure she was blushing, and didn't know whether to stay put or run for the exit. "I…I've…got to go check on the car. Do you want to—? Well, never mind—I'll be back in a minute…" She sprinted away, leaving Chris with a puzzled look on his face.

Outside, Kenzie shook off her confusion and looked for her beloved Jeep Cherokee, a forest green, no-frills 1990 model handed down from her mom. Kenzie took a perverse pride in not having a brand-new BMW convertible or a $50,000 Range Rover, especially since her family could easily afford to buy them for all the kids. The Dawsons' lack of ostentation, as well as their quiet philanthropy, were two things Kenzie appreciated most about her family.

Behind the Jeep, a dour-faced airport cop had his foot on the rear bumper, as he scribbled down the license number for yet another ticket.

I'm going to kill Allie, thought Kenzie. *Okay, time for the old Dawson charm...*

"Uh, hi, Officer. I am *so* sorry. I wasn't really parking. You see, my friend is picking us up, and she really *did* park in the garage. She was just pulling up to load our luggage, and it's not here yet..."

Kenzie poured it on thick, playing up the soft Southern drawl that never failed to charm those around her—especially men.

"It's been here too long," said the officer, without smiling. "You're not supposed to park here."

"But Officer, I, we—Well, my friends played this really great joke on me and my friend Ethan, you see, because we're from Tennessee. They brought a banjo player and everything... would you like to hear him?"

Tucking his ticket book under one arm and scratching his chin, the policeman tilted his head at Kenzie and said, "Nashville, Tennessee? Grand Ole Opry and all that?" He broke into a grin. "Ha! You know Johnny Cash?"

Kenzie didn't expect this. She hoped against hope that her friends were still waiting for the luggage.

"Well, you won't believe this, but actually...my dad knows him. My dad used to play at the Opry..."

"Are you kidding me? I used to listen to the Opry on the radio when I was a kid, back in north Florida. What's your daddy's name? Maybe I heard of him."

"Johnny Dawson. He wasn't like a big star or anything—"

"Jumpin' Johnny Dawson? From Elvis's band? You're kiddin' me! I'm a huge Elvis fan!"

"That's my dad," Kenzie said, sheepishly. She quickly changed the subject. "Um, am I gonna get a ticket? I promise we're leaving any minute now."

"Well, kid, just because you're Johnny Dawson's girl, I'll let you off. This time. In honor of Elvis, and Jumpin' Johnny. Just don't leave it parked, all right?

"Yes, sir, I promise—Oh, here come my friends! Okay, we're leaving, really..." Kenzie breathed a sigh of relief as the policeman was distracted by a near-wreck on the other side of the parking lot, just when her friends started piling into the Cherokee. They crammed luggage, instruments, six freshmen and an anonymous banjo player into the back of the Jeep, taking up every inch of available space.

"Somebody's got to sit on a lap!" Allie announced, winking at Kenzie.

To Kenzie's relief, Chris was folded up in the very back, with his guitar already cradled in his lap. Cooper took the opportunity to slide onto Ryan's knees with practiced ease and a happy grin.

Hmmm, Kenzie thought. *They seem to be getting along pretty well. I wouldn't have put those two together, but he's a great guy. Then again, so is Chris...*

As Kenzie cranked the engine and pulled away from the curb, she heard the voice of the airport cop through her open window.

"Say hello to Elvis for me, next time you're in Tennessee! He's still alive, you know!"

"I will! Thank you, sir!" Kenzie yelled her response and whipped the Jeep into the flow of traffic to avoid any more revealing conversation.

"What? What did he say? Did he say something about Elvis?" Allie yelled into Kenzie's ear over all the chatter and Chris' guitar picking. "Is that guy wacko or what?"

"Yeah...it was the Tennessee license plate, probably. But *I almost got a ticket*, thanks to you, Allie!" Kenzie steered the conversation as easily as she steered the Jeep into traffic.

"'Almost'? What'd you do? Turn on the Southern charm? And he let you off? I've got to learn a Southern accent. You get out of *everything!*"

"Aside from helping me get away with a few things, a Southern accent's not worth too much else. I wish I had your husky voice, Al! Guys dig that, you know. But…tell you what; I'll teach you Southern charm, if you teach me to speak Indian."

"That's highly unlikely. Besides, it's called Hindi, not 'Indian,' and it's very difficult. I'm not sure you're up to the intellectual challenge," she said, smiling.

Kenzie reached over and delivered a solid, good-natured slug to Allie's upper arm. As she did, she caught a glimpse of Chris in the rear-view mirror, with his head bent low over his guitar so he could hear it over the chatter. She saw his lips moving; he was singing. She wondered what song it was and if she knew it. Suddenly, he looked up and caught her eye in the rear-view mirror. Her heart skipped a beat as he smiled at her reflection, then went back to his song.

She straightened up quickly, mortified that he had caught her staring at him.

"Uh-oh, Allie. Bad news."

"What?"

"He just caught me staring at him in the mirror. I can't recover. The damage is done. It's over."

She tried to concentrate on driving, but her thoughts kept drifting back to Chris and the possibility of seeing him play that night at The Cup and Chaucer.

Kenzie shook her head as if to clear it. That would be later. The first order of business was getting the gang to change out of their hillbilly outfits. She and Ethan had loved the joke. But, like most Tennesseans, they could quickly become weary of the goofy, "Hee-Haw" stereotype.

Snaking the Jeep around the hilly curves on the edge of the PCU campus, Kenzie began to feel a little queasy once again. A propensity for motion sickness was the bane of her existence, and it precluded a number of activities that matched her zest for adventure. All her life, Kenzie had kept trying: flying lessons (she hurled on her first try), a Bahamas cruise (over the starboard side, twice), even fast rollercoasters. Needless to say, amusement park dates were a problem.

Her excellent driving skills had been cultivated partially out of necessity, when Kenzie's dad decided to let her do all the family driving as soon as she got her license, rather than risk getting a queasy passenger.

But sometimes even driving got to her, especially driving on winding streets. Compounded by all the excitement, her lack of sleep, and the fact that she'd lost her breakfast on the flight, Kenzie was suddenly ready to get out of the car and lie down. At this point, even the suite's avocado green sofa sounded good.

"Hey, I hate to break up the party, but can I take y'all home? I really need to take a nap or something." Kenzie pulled into the quad where the guys' dorms were, hoping to unload Drew, Ryan, Ethan, the still-anonymous banjo player, and Chris.

Chris…oh, my gosh. Should I ask him if he's playing at The Cup tonight or should I wait and see if he says anything to me about it? He is so cute…

Kenzie's slightly queasy stomach got even queasier at the thought of admitting she was romantically interested in a musician. Thankfully, her musings were interrupted by laughter and the sounds of Jeep doors opening.

"Sure, Kenz…you must be tired, huh? Glad you guys are

back," said Drew, enthusiastically.

Like Allie, Drew had become part of the crowd late in the previous semester, after Kenzie got involved in the Young Life leadership group. Drew was fun, and the cutest of the guys in their little gang—he reminded Kenzie of her Green Hills Academy classmates back home, guys with too much money, who helped foot the bill every place they went, just to keep the fun going.

"Hey, Allie, good job! Thanks for asking me," said Drew. "Are you guys going to The Cup tonight? Chris is playing. Aren't you, Chris? Chris?"

But Chris was already halfway across the quad lawn, walking toward the dorm with his soft-side guitar case hitched over his right shoulder.

"Oh, well." Drew shrugged. "Guess he's writing a song in his head or something. Well, see you guys later."

Easing herself down from the Jeep, Kenzie stepped over her carry-on flight bag and two suitcases, which had mysteriously appeared at her feet. Perplexed, she looked around to see who'd put them there.

"Ethan, did you do this for me? That's nice. Thanks."

"Wasn't me," he said quietly, as he gathered his own bags. Now that he was back among the crowd, he was also back to being the quiet Ethan everyone saw, rather than the talkative guy only Kenzie seemed to know. *Must be the "sister" thing,* Kenzie thought. *That, or the fact that he's seen me blow chunks. That's always a bonding moment between friends.*

Allie grabbed Kenzie's arm and whispered, "Chris got your bags. I saw him." She grinned mischievously and piped up loud enough for all to hear, "So, you're buying for everyone tonight, don't forget. I'm sure John and Peg loaded you up with Christmas bucks, so you can spend some of it on us. Of course, if Chris plays tonight, he gets his lattés free. Maybe he'll give you one."

"Whatever," said Kenzie. "You won't believe it, but a latté does not sound good right now. I need a Vernor's. As if I could find one on this campus! Unless there's one stashed in the fridge at our suite." She hoped so. A nice cold ginger ale would soothe her stomach and give her the little kick she needed to wake up. Or maybe a nap was in order.

"Kenzie?" It was Ethan, looking kind of cute in his wire-rimmed glasses and flannel shirt.

"I'll carry your stuff up, then go park your car for you, if you want. Go crash."

"You're the best, E," said Kenzie. She pulled him beside her and whispered, "Sorry I urped on you, on the flight this morning. You were sweet."

That's what he was, of course. Sweet. Brotherly. A friend. Always there for Kenzie when she needed him. But the chemistry wasn't there. She knew she wouldn't want to kiss him. Somebody would, though, she hoped. He deserved someone special.

"You didn't urp *on* me, Kenz, you urped *near* me. Big difference. Now go take a nap."

Kenzie felt the urge to give him a quick hug, and so she did. Getting hugged was not a regular thing for the bashful Ethan, but he always appreciated it and hugged back.

"Thanks again, E. See you at The Cup?"

"Yep. It oughta be a good show, if you know what I mean." He pulled his glasses to the end of his nose and peered over them at Kenzie.

"Oh, hush. You're a goob, Ethan." So much for brother-sister tenderness. He was giving her grief about Chris, and she knew it.

Kenzie walked slowly across the quad, taking in as much of the scenery as she could in her state of nausea. She loved PCU. It had the aesthetics of an Ivy League school—steeped in tradition, with its old brick-and-stone buildings tucked amid the evergreens. It was just a short walk from the bustling heart of Seattle's "U-District," named for the University of Washington and PCU campuses, full of trendy shops, restaurants, bookstores, art movie houses, and ubiquitous coffeehouses.

That's where her little gang of freshmen would be tonight—having fun, getting to know each other, enjoying the freedom of being away from Mom and Dad—college life just they way they'd dreamed of it. At The Cup, they'd be full of stories from Christmas break, happy to be back at school again from all over—Connecticut, Oregon, California, Colorado, and yes, the great state of Tennessee. And, oddly, only one native Washingtonian, from Moses Lake, in the eastern part of the state. *That would be Chris…*

Lost in thought, Kenzie found herself at the entrance to her dorm building. Opening the door, she was greeted with the smells of musty hallways, stale popcorn, and a faint hint of institutional disinfectant. She smiled. *I'm home. Kind of.*

Kenzie dragged herself to the suite and flopped on her bed without taking off her boots, or even bothering to check the fridge for a Vernor's. *Too tired…gotta rest up for tonight…at The Cup…with Chris…*

3

sleep on her narrow dorm bed, surrounded by favorite teddy bears and stuffed bunnies, Kenzie Dawson drifted pleasantly through Dreamland. Banjos, bad hillbilly tunes and chatty airport cops were far from her consciousness, as were the busy streets of Seattle and the ivy-covered brick environs of Pacific Cascades University. In their place were the snow-capped peaks surrounding Malibu, Young Life's teen resort tucked away in the beautiful Princess Louisa Inlet of British Columbia.

In her dream, it was summer, and Kenzie wore a pair of nylon running shorts and a Young Life T-shirt. She was running down the boardwalk, down the hill from the cabins, past the tall, colorful totem poles left by the Native Americans who'd lived in the area for milleniums. The sun was out, and it shone upon the water, where kids waterskied, swam, and sailed—all while screaming with delight.

Running past the last totem pole before the dock, Kenzie looked up and saw that carved into it was the face of Dylan Frost, the 20-year-old musician from Nashville, who Kenzie had dated briefly during the summer of her junior year in high school. Dylan was artistic, rebellious, and very romantic. When Kenzie knew him, he didn't have a "real job." To Dylan, settling for anything less than a music career would have meant "selling out."

Perhaps because he was so unlike the Green Hills Academy guys she knew, or maybe because Kenzie had found herself searching for something that year, she had been taken in by Dylan's "tortured artist" persona. He was hard to resist, with his big brown doe eyes, romantic gestures and breathless, poetic entreaties. Despite her best intentions—and all the good Billy Weber songs she'd heard about being true to one's convictions —Kenzie had given in to some of Dylan's pleas for physical intimacy. Yet she drew the line before they got into real trouble. Although she knew at least half of the girls in her school had already had sex by age sixteen, Kenzie really did believe in waiting for marriage. However, after her brief relationship with Dylan, Kenzie was still left with the regret of having compromised some important principles.

In Kenzie's dream, the sight of Dylan's face in the totem pole was alarming. She ran harder and harder down the hill until she got to the dock. There, moored to the launch, Kenzie found not a ski boat, but a huge, hollowed-out guitar, with its sail billowing in the wind. Standing on the dock, ready to launch the boat/guitar, was Chris Gallagher, dressed in a captain's outfit, with a white uniform, jaunty white cap, and epaulets on the shoulders. He called Kenzie's name and gestured, inviting her onto the boat.

"I can't," she said. "I have to buy a life jacket first. I can't swim; I've tried before and I almost drowned." Captain Chris assured her that he already had a life jacket on the boat, and that she was safe with him.

Still, she hesitated, and as she did, the boat/guitar began to slip away, with Chris on board, waving, waving...

"Kenzie! Kenzie! Wake up! You're going to miss it!"

Out of the murky depths of exhausted sleep, Kenzie heard a familiar voice. It was Emily.

"Wha—? Huh? What time is it?" Kenzie eased open her eyes and groggily surveyed the darkened room.

"It's 7:45! You've been asleep for hours, and you've already missed dinner! Cooper and I figured we'd better not wake you up for that, but you can't miss The Cup and Chaucer. Maybe you can get a bagel there—it's been a long time since you ate. Are you okay?"

"Yeah, I'm okay. Um, where's, where's...um, never mind. Did you guys eat yet?" Kenzie was trying hard to focus on her suite-mate's face.

"I thought I just told you that," said Emily, flipping on the overhead light, which made Kenzie squint. "Sorry. We were hoping to have a suite dinner, first day back. Who knows where Beth is, though. Are you starved?"

"Uh...yeah. Sure. Hold on a minute and let me wake up. I just had the weirdest dream..."

"Well, no offense or anything, but you might want to change clothes. You're kind of wrinkled. So tell me about the dream." Emily was eager for a little insight into the mind of her normally outgoing roommate, who was often uncharacteristically reserved around Emily.

"Oh, it wasn't anything," said Kenzie. She was still wondering about it herself, and she wasn't about to offer her dream for Emily's Psych 101 analysis. "Really, no big deal. So what was for dinner, anyhow?"

"Mexican," said Emily, clearly disappointed at Kenzie's unwillingness to spill the beans. "Fajitas, I think, with chicken and beef and stuff. It was really pretty good."

"That's a switch." Like nearly everyone else at PCU, Kenzie felt the need to make snide comments about the quality of the campus cafeteria food, even though it was far better than what most were expecting. It was way better than high school cafeteria food. But not as good as the food at Malibu. *Wonder why in the world I dreamed about Malibu?* thought Kenzie. *And Dylan? And Chris...and that boat/guitar. Weird. Very weird.*

"It wasn't the best I've had, but it wasn't bad," said Cooper, who'd come in and plopped herself down on the edge of Kenzie's bed. "Kenzie, I'm sorry, but you aren't going anywhere looking like that. I cannot, in good conscience, let you out of the suite."

"Okay, I'm changing, I'm changing—oh, no! My clothes are still in the suitcase. They'll all be wrinkled, anyway."

"You can wear something of mine!" laughed Cooper. "If you have the nerve."

The thought of being seen at The Cup and Chaucer in Cooper's out-there New York stuff was a little too much for the preppy Kenzie to bear.

"Thanks anyway, *chiquita*. I must have left something here from before Christmas." Kenzie pawed through the small closet she shared with Beth, the continually absent roommate Kenzie called "The Phantom."

Beth's clothes didn't take up much room. Kenzie figured she must have moved most of them to her boyfriend's house in nearby Tacoma, since she apparently spent most nights there. Many mornings last semester, Kenzie would wake up to find Beth arriving at the room in time to change clothes and race to her 8:00 class. On the rare occasions when Beth and Kenzie were in the room together, their conversation rarely got past the surface. Kenzie didn't feel comfortable asking personal questions—there really hadn't been enough time. Now, as she surveyed the almost-empty closet, Kenzie wondered if she had been too cautious about asking those kinds of questions.

She pulled a clean pair of Levis from a hanger and found a seafoam-green cashmere sweater that looked good with her hair. *Wonder if this is too dressy for The Cup,* she thought. *Maybe not with jeans…well, anyway, Mom would be proud…I wonder if Chris really is going to play. And why in the heck was he in that freaky dream? Maybe I'll ask Allie about it…Allie…oh yeah, she's gonna make me buy for everyone tonight…Where's that Christmas cash?*

"Hey, roomies—did Ethan bring my backpack in? My wallet's in it."

"In here," yelled Cooper, from the living room. "I'll bring it to you."

Cooper appeared in Kenzie's room, bearing the backpack.

"Well, look at you! A cashmere sweater? I've never seen you in cashmere. And lipstick? What's the occasion? Expecting to see someone?"

"No," said Kenzie, lying through her teeth. "This is the only thing I have that's not wrinkled. And I always wear lipstick at night. It's the law where I come from. So…what? Do I look too dressed up for Seattle?" Kenzie hardly considered Cooper the arbiter of good fashion sense, but she *was* from New York.

"You look fine. In fact, you look *too* fine. Do me a favor and stay away from Ryan, okay?"

Kenzie laughed, remembering the cozy scene on the way back from the airport, with Cooper on Ryan's lap. He was smitten with Cooper, that much was obvious.

"Not to worry, Coop. If I showed up at The Cup in a red, strapless dress, he probably wouldn't even notice. You could be wearing a Mariners uniform and he'd still be watching you."

"That's an idea. Hey, could I wear your Mariners cap? Might be fun."

"You, in a baseball cap? Miss Athletically Impaired? This I gotta see. Sure, go ahead. But don't wear it like a dork." Kenzie grabbed the cap from the floor, where it had fallen when she'd rolled over during her long nap. She clapped it on Cooper's head.

"No, don't try to straighten out the bill. A straight bill is very *wrong*." Kenzie demonstrated the proper technique for ballcap wearing.

"Where did you get this, anyway, Kenzie? I think you had this on the day I met you, before orientation. Isn't this a Seattle thing?"

The cap had been a gift from Christian pop star Billy Weber, Kenzie's family friend. But Kenzie wasn't about to tell Cooper—or anyone, for that matter—that Billy had brought it back after he sang the national anthem at a Mariners game in the Seattle Kingdome.

"Uh, yeah, it is. Friend of ours brought it back to me from a business trip." *That's not a lie,* thought Kenzie. *It was a business trip...Billy's just not your average businessman, that's all.*

"Cool. I think it looks pretty good on me, don't you?" Cooper admired herself in Kenzie's mirror. The ball cap looked remarkably fashionable on Cooper.

"You GUYS! Are we going or not?" Emily appeared from the hallway, wearing a rain parka and jeans. "Wow! Kenzie, you look great! Are you trying to impress someone tonight?" Cooper gave Kenzie a knowing look and pushed the ball cap toward the back of her head.

"Emily, Kenzie claims this is the only unwrinkled thing she has. Personally, I think she's got something up her sleeve. Like scamming on Drew, maybe."

"Drew? Wrong," said Kenzie. "Too much like the guys back home. Whattya think I came all the way out here for? I'm telling ya, if he had a Southern accent, he'd fit right in at my high school."

Drew Ragsdale was just the kind of boy Kenzie and her friends at home would have dated: preppy, cute, athletic. He reminded her of the guys who vacationed with their families at Vail, Beaver Creek, and Telluride, and had their own ski stuff —even though they only skied a couple of times a year.

Drew seemed a likely obvious choice for Kenzie, being so much like the boys back home. Chris, on the other hand, wasn't like any guy she'd known, with the exception of her friend Billy Weber, and Billy didn't count because he was twenty years older and married besides. Like Billy, Kenzie knew, Chris was a sensitive musician, who could be kind of spacey and pre-occupied when he was playing his guitar or sitting at a piano keyboard. But, like Billy, Chris also was sincere and seemed responsible. Billy had worked in a warehouse to pay the rent for his family before he got his first songwriting contract; Chris was determined to get his degree and just play music on the side.

That was the scoop, anyway. Kenzie had received all of her information secondhand; she'd been too standoffish with him to get too far beyond superficial conversation. Kenzie still wasn't ready to reveal her ties with the music industry. Worrying that if they got to talking about his musical dreams, she'd feel too guilty about hiding her "insider" status, she generally avoided the issue.

"Dang, he's cute, though…" Kenzie muttered under her breath. She stared absentmindedly at her reflection in the mirror over her dresser, lost in thoughts about Chris.

"Drew?" asked Cooper. "Totally! I'd be after him, if I didn't have Ryan, who is a major babe, if you ask me."

Emily made a face like she'd just sucked on a lemon.

"Cooper! Yuck! It kinda grosses me out when you talk about my brother that way."

"Sorry. Aren't you used to that by now, though? Didn't you know the girls he went out with in high school?"

Emily's face was still slightly contorted with a look of disgust. "Yes, but I never had to *live* with his girlfriends and watch them make out with him on the couch in *my* living room! Blegghh!"

Cooper looked hurt. "*When* have you ever seen us make out on the couch?"

"Okay, so I haven't. But it could happen." Emily laughed. "Just make sure I'm in class or something, okay?"

Cooper kept on. "Out with it, Emily—are you afraid the big-city girl is going to corrupt your all-American, small-town hero brother? I may be from Manhattan, but I've got the same morals you do."

Emily looked chagrined. "Well, I have to admit, you're really different than all the girls at our high school. But you're cool. I was mostly kidding. Maybe you could get married and then you'd be my sister-in-law. Wouldn't that be the best?!" Suddenly, everything was peachy. Kenzie couldn't help but think that Emily didn't deal with conflict very well.

"Oh, *brother!* You are both such geeks!" Kenzie rolled her eyes and threw a jacket over her cashmere sweater. "Let's GO! They're going to run out of foam for the lattés down there. Plus, Allie's going to wonder where the cash cow is."

Outside the ivy-covered dorm, the rain fell softly. The weather was no big surprise to the girls. Kenzie was used to Southern rains, even in the summer, and Emily was from Oregon, where it rained almost as much as it did in Seattle. Cooper had said that she was used to rain, but Kenzie had her doubts.

"Cooper, how could you even tell? Don't you live in a twenty-story apartment house or something like that? Do you even go outside?"

This time it was Cooper who rolled her eyes. "I'm not even answering that. New Yorkers walk everywhere, you know—not like you suburbanites, with your Jeeps and car phones." Cooper smiled, so Kenzie would know she was just giving her grief.

"Wait a minute, I have to defend myself! I do *not* have a car phone. I'm *so* over that. My dad, however, has a cellphone permanently attached to his right hand," said Kenzie. "Even on vacation, until my mom turns it off and hides it from him."

"So what does he do that's so important?" asked Emily, casually.

Oops. Kenzie cleared her throat, realizing she had almost spilled the beans to the one person on campus who would care the most about what her dad did. *Emily, Miss Christian Music Freak. There's so much to like about her, except for that...and I'm the only one bothered by it.*

"Oh, he's just your average corporate exec kinda guy. Always thinking about business. I love him, though...he's the best. So, Cooper, where is Ryan, anyway?" *Whew. That was a close one.*

"He said he had to study, and that he would meet us there later."

"Study?" Kenzie was incredulous. "The semester hasn't even started yet!"

Emily piped up with a sisterly defense. "He pre-registered at the end of last semester and bought the books after finals from a kid who needed Christmas cash. Cheaper than the bookstore."

"But study? On the first night back from break? Sheesh." Kenzie still couldn't believe it. "He's such an edge."

"Edge?" Emily wanted clarification.

"Short for education freak. You know, like brainiac, egghead…that's what we called studious types in Nashville."

"Like you weren't one yourself! You had to be, to get into PCU." Cooper was joining Emily in sticking up for her boyfriend.

"I don't study before the semester starts, for cryin' out loud! Do you?"

"No, but I didn't get a full academic scholarship like Ryan, either. And he does have a life, you know."

"I'm kidding," said Kenzie, grinning. "Well, we're about to find out if Mr. Edge got his nose out of the books to see his girl-friend."

The girls had laughed and chatted their way across campus in the rain, shielding their hair with jackets lifted above their heads. From the cold, wet streets of the University District, the lights from the windows of The Cup and Chaucer looked especially warm and inviting. As they approached, the sound of familiar laughter brought smiles to all three—the hearty, child-like giggle-guffaw of Kenzie's best friend at PCU.

"Allie. You can always tell where she is, with that goofy laugh."

Kenzie looked in the window and waved at her pal. "Hey, there's Ryan, Coop. He just saw me, and now he's totally looking for you. See what I mean? Nothing to worry about."

"Maybe he's worried about his precious baby sister," Emily suggested.

"Yeah, right, Em," said Kenzie. "I know I don't have any brothers, but I still know better than that."

"He really does worry about me, you know," Emily said, with a slight pout. "Too much, sometimes. Drives me crazy."

"Well, he's not worried about you right now, obviously."

Ryan burst through the outside door and greeted Cooper with a hug and a quick kiss. "Hey, girls! We've been waiting for you! Especially you, Kenzie—Allie says you're buying." Ryan winked at Kenzie.

"In her dreams! Not after the Unfortunate Hillbilly Incident at the airport."

Kenzie loved using that phrase as much as possible: as in the "Unfortunate Hurling Incident" for which she had apologized to Ethan. *Was that today? I can't believe it*, thought Kenzie. *What a day. What a nap. What a weird dream. I wonder if Chris is here.*

Holding the door open for the girls, Ryan said something that made Kenzie wonder if he was reading her mind.

"Chris doesn't start playing till nine tonight, but he'll be here soon. Come on over! Maddy's here."

At a grouping of comfortable chairs and couches sat Ethan, Drew, and Allie. Next to them, perched on the arm of an over-stuffed chair, was Maddy MacDonald, a wacky, free-spirited freshman who worked nights at The Cup. Maddy was one of Kenzie's favorite people at PCU, not just because she made lattés the way Kenzie liked them, but because she never worried about what other people thought.

The laughter was interrupted as Kenzie and her suite-mates plopped down on several nearby chairs.

"Hey!" yelled Allie, jumping up to hug them all. "Where have you been? I told everyone Kenzie was buying, remember? We've been deprived now for an hour, drinking water."

"Mm-hmm. I can see that," said Kenzie, sarcastically, as she surveyed the mess of half-finished cappuccinos and Blue Sky soda bottles. *Ethan's*, she thought. *He's not too sure about these coffee drinks. I bet Drew bought everybody a round already.*

"Great sweater, Kenzie," said Drew, in his usual charming

way. "You look great in it, I mean." Kenzie wondered if someone, his mother maybe, had told him to always compliment the person, not the clothing item. *Well, good for him for remembering. Some guys talk like they want to date a girl's closet.*

"It is nice," Allie agreed, casually enough. "Kind of nice just for The Cup. Are you going somewhere after here? Hmmm?" Kenzie considered giving Allie the evil eye, but thought better of it in front of their friends.

"No. I just felt like wearing it," Kenzie said innocently. "It's a free country."

"Um, how're you feeling, Kenzie?" Ethan voiced his question quietly, sensitive to the fact that she made him promise not to tell about her airplane illness.

"Oh, you mean tossing my cookies on the plane?" Kenzie said it loud enough for everyone to hear, much to Ethan's confusion.

"Kenzie, why didn't you tell us you got sick? You looked fine at the airport," said Allie, looking somewhat concerned.

"I hurled, all right. Major hurlage. Totally embarrassing. Didn't make it to the little airplane bathroom, either."

At this point, Kenzie was on a roll. When it came to telling a good story, with an audience, embarrassment easily took a back seat to entertainment.

"You poor thing!" said Emily, sympathetically.

"Did you have to blow in the bag?" Drew was relishing the moment.

"Yep. Perfectly. Poor Ethan—what a pal! Fortunately, I didn't hurl directly on him. But you know, this was nothing compared to my flight to Europe last summer. I hurled nine times from New York to London," Kenzie said dramatically. "Basically barfed all the way across the ocean. A transatlantic hurl, if you will. But I got to use the oxygen tank, and the flight attendants let me stay back in the galley with them."

Kenzie was in full swing by now, and her friends were right with her: the guys appreciating a girl who could talk so freely about such things, the girls sympathizing with her horrifying story.

Kenzie sat on the back of an armchair and continued to entertain her friends with tales of her favorite "Unfortunate Hurling Incidents." Right in the middle of one of her best stories, however, she got a funny feeling in the pit of her stomach. Looking up, she found herself face to face with the one person at PCU whose very presence could cause her to blush. She had no idea how long he'd been standing there, with his soft, black guitar bag slung over his shoulder.

But Chris Gallagher looked very, very amused.

4

Kenzie should have been mortified. But somehow, she was only slightly embarrassed. That night, Chris laughed right along with her gross-out stories. He intrigued her so much, she ended up staying out way too late and drank way too many lattés, in a not-so-subtle effort to catch every one of the songs he played that night.

So it was no surprise, in the days that followed, when her friends started teasing her about her budding friendship with Chris. Cooper and Emily were especially merciless, and on the occasions that the elusive Beth showed up, she got enough ammunition from the others to jump in and tease Kenzie on her own.

Kenzie, herself, was a master kidder. But, somehow, this time the joking was getting to her, and she wasn't sure why. She wondered if it was because this thing with Chris was different from any crush she'd experienced before.

After that crazy, disturbing dream she'd had, she was starting to analyze the similarities and differences between Chris and her old boyfriend, the "flaky musician," Dylan Frost.

Kenzie knew that something was going on inside her, and she didn't know how to work it out. But one thing was for sure: she wasn't going to bring it up around the suite. Emily and Cooper were both taking Psych 101, and the last thing Kenzie wanted was a Freudian dream analysis from either one of them. Especially Emily.

As much as Kenzie hated to see it in herself, she was keeping Emily at as much of a distance as was politely possible. And the longer she lived with Emily, the more she realized how unfair it was. Emily really was a good person, and it was clear that she wanted to be closer with Kenzie. Sometimes, when Em left in the morning to go running with her friend Zoey, Kenzie thought about how much she was missing, how her fears were keeping her from enjoying a good friendship.

Allie, on the other hand, was safe.

One afternoon, in a hidden, dusty corner in the "stacks" section on the second floor of the library, Kenzie interrupted their studies to finally begin the process of spilling the beans, one little bean at a time.

"Allie?" Kenzie whispered.

Allie looked up from her textbook. "Yes?"

"Hey, um…" Kenzie's whisper was barely audible. "Do you think that…well, do you know anything about…well…"

"Can't hear you. Spit it out. What's going on?" Allie perked up and looked at Kenzie sideways, like a curious puppy."

"Okay…do you know anything about dreams? I mean, I had a totally weird one, and my old boyfriend was in it, sort of, and it was at Malibu, and Chris was in it, and there was a boat, but it was a guitar, and I was running, and—"

"Wait! Hold on, girl! One bizarre dream item at a time," said Allie, trying to keep her voice down. "You were at Malibu? And which boyfriend?"

"Dylan. The musician. Well, his face was on a totem pole, down by the dock, you know?" What does that mean?" Kenzie furrowed her brow in concentration.

"Dylan's face…we'll get to that in a minute. First things first —Chris showed up in your dream? This means, you know, that you're finally accepting the fact that you're attracted to him. It's about time, I might add," said Allie smugly.

Kenzie looked at her in dismay. "Is it really obvious? People are starting to give me grief about it. Especially you, thank you very much."

Allie slammed her French textbook shut, using both hands to great dramatic effect.

"This is not something that should be discussed in a library, Kenz. We need to be in a booth somewhere, having ourselves a warm beverage."

"The Cup? Are you nuts? And see everybody we know? *Wrong*. How about the Daily Grind, at the SUB?" Kenzie suggested, referring to the student union building. "That's a totally uncool place for coffee. No one we know would be hanging around."

"Good idea. I have to check my mail, anyway," said Allie, stuffing books in her leather backpack.

The two left the library and headed across the broad expanse of lawn.

Since it was the middle of the afternoon, the SUB was fairly quiet. Kenzie and Allie stopped in the lobby to check the bulletin board for exciting campus news, found none, and made their way to the campus post office. The post office, located in the basement of the union, was a low-ceilinged, dull alcove comprised of stark walls lined with endless rows of gray metal cubbyholes.

Allie jammed her key in box 1361 and pulled it open.

Inside, she found a J. Crew catalog and a notice about a campus-wide blood drive.

"That's the pits. No letters. No one writes letters anymore. Not even my mother. What'd you get?"

As soon as the words left Allie's mouth, a familiar voice piped up behind Kenzie's shoulder as she was struggling to open her box.

"Hey, guys! Did you get anything good? Let's hope my mom sent cookies. I'd share!"

It was Emily, being her usual cheery self, which grated on Kenzie's nerves sometimes. This was one of those times, and Kenzie felt guilty about it, as usual.

"Oh, look, Kenzie! Cool! You've got a package slip! Wonder what it is?"

"We'll see…" With a feeling of dread, Kenzie handed the slip of paper to the disinterested student behind the counter. After fishing through a huge bin, the worker came up with a large brown padded envelope, bearing a corporate logo.

"Cool! What is it?" Emily wondered aloud.

"Probably clothes or something I ordered," said Kenzie, stuffing the envelope into her backpack. "No big deal."

Emily had heard this before from Kenzie, and Kenzie felt guilty about the guise. But Kenzie also knew that if Emily found out that those mysterious packages were the latest CDs from her dad's Christian record company, she could make Kenzie's life miserable.

"How 'bout you, Em?" Though it was Kenzie's unconscious habit to shorten the names of all her friends, she did it quite intentionally this time, in an effort to make Emily feel closer than Kenzie really wanted her to be. She hoped that would compensate for the irrational distance Kenzie put between them.

"A letter from my friend, Holly. But no cookies. Hey, do you guys know Billy Weber? Well, of course you do, Kenzie—I play his CD all the time—and have his poster in my room, of course. Anyway, they just announced on the Christian radio station that he's coming to Seattle next month! I'm so excited! Maybe we could get a bunch of people to go!"

Kenzie went pale. How did she miss the news that their family friend, the Christian pop star, was doing a concert in Seattle? *Why didn't Dad tell me this was coming up?*

"Yeah, I know who he is...that's cool, Em. Are you going to promote the concert on your radio show? Maybe you should do a Billy-a-Thon or something, pick your top-twenty Billy Weber favorites and count 'em down. 'All Billy, All the Time with Emily Stewart on 91 Rock' or something like that." Kenzie hoped her suggestions didn't sound cynical.

"That's an awesome idea! Do you want to help me with it?" Emily lit up at the thought.

Oh no. I was only trying to be friendly, and now I've got myself in deep.

Kenzie shook her head and laughed nervously. "I don't think you'd want me to, Em, trust me! I just gave you all the creative juice I had. But I'm sure you'll do great."

Kenzie shifted her backpack on her shoulder and pulled her thick hair out from under the strap. *If she only knew...I could set her up with CDs to give away on the air, a phone interview with Billy, free passes. She could have a killer show if I was willing to help...but I'm not going to think about that right now...*

"Well, that's a great idea you gave me. Thanks! I'm going to go figure out my top-twenty favorites right now. Oh, you didn't say—do you guys want to go to the concert? I could be in charge of getting tickets for everyone—"

Allie spoke up. "Sounds good, Emily. Find out how much

tickets are and let me know." She shot a glance at Kenzie, who glared back at her.

"I'm not sure, Em…I'll get back to you on that. Allie, we gotta go—see ya at the suite, Bunkie?" She was reaching for an out, and hoped the affectionate term for her suite-mate would do the trick.

"Sure! See ya later!" Emily smiled sunnily as Kenzie and Allie took their leave.

"Oh, great, Al. Now what am I going to do? I wish they'd warned me about this." Kenzie's bright blue eyes darkened under her furrowed brows.

"Warn you? Kenz, your dad and your friend Billy have no clue that you're living a double life out here! Telling Emily 'yeah, I know who he is'—girl, you're gonna have to let the cat out of the bag pretty soon. Maybe it won't be so bad. Maybe it won't be that big of a deal to Emily." Allie was walking fast to keep up with Kenzie, who turned into an Olympic racewalker when she was tense about something.

"Yeah, right. She's going to squeal like a stuck pig," said Kenzie.

"Excuse me, there's the hillbilly coming out in you again. Can you translate, please? We don't raise pigs in Silicon Valley." Allie was trying to defuse the tension with laughter.

"I guess it's a Southern expression. But, c'mon, you get the picture. Anyway, Emily is just so into Christian music, and she'll want to gherm Billy if she knows I know him…ohhhh… this could be awful."

"Gherm? Translation, please," said Allie.

"You know…like groupie. It's a noun and a verb, both. Don't ask me where it came from. You "gherm" somebody famous when you go up to 'em at a restaurant and tell them that you love their music or whatever. Happens to Billy all the time."

"Oh, like you wouldn't 'gherm' Brad Pitt if you saw him at The Cup and Chaucer?"

"Hey, why don't we go to The Cup anyway?" Allie suggested. "We still have to analyze your dream. Nobody'll be there. It's four o'clock. And would you slow *down?*" Allie yanked at Kenzie's leather jacket like she was applying the brakes on a runaway train.

"Okay...but I've got to figure out what to do about Billy's concert. Maybe I can be out of town that weekend," said Kenzie, grimacing.

"Yeah, right. For what? And to where? You just have to suck it up and handle this," said Allie. "Besides, it's about time you did. It's not like you could hide this all four years. And what about Chris? If you really start dating him, you're going to have to 'fess up, and you *know* you could help him get started in the music business. In a *serious* way!"

Kenzie's countenance dropped even further. She had thought that her friend Allie, of all people, would understand why she *couldn't* tell Chris. If he found out that her dad was one of the most influential people in Christian music, it could ruin everything. Not that he'd take advantage of that; he had no idea that he was talented enough to "make it" in music. Writing those songs and playing for people was his passion, but Kenzie had a feeling he barely even dreamed about doing it for a living. And yet, something in her longed to help him fulfill his potential.

"Kenzie? Hello? Are you in there?" Allie looked quizzically at her friend.

"Uh, sorry. Allie, do you understand what's at stake here? Like my whole life. Like being able to be a normal person, instead of Johnny Dawson's daughter. Do you even get that?" Kenzie's irritated tone produced a hurt look on her friend's lovely brown, East Indian face.

"Of course I do! I know a little bit about living up to expectations, you know. Being the daughter of two brilliant Stanford computer-sci professors is hard, too—especially since I didn't get their math and science genes—which is why I'm at PCU instead of Stanford or Cal Tech or MIT."

Kenzie's brow relaxed, and she even cracked a smile.

"Sorry...you do have it pretty rough, being the mathematically challenged offspring of the Doctors Raju. Are you sure you're not adopted?" Kenzie loved teasing her friend Allie about her lopsided SAT scores, which reflected her extraordinary verbal abilities and her even-less-than-ordinary math skills, a point which had caused much consternation in the Raju household.

"If I didn't look like an exact fifty-fifty version of my mom and dad, I'd wonder," said Allie. "But enough about my weird parents. Let's talk about your weird dream. And by the way, I do understand about your double life. Of course I do. I just have a feeling it's about to end."

By force of habit as much as anything, the two found their Olympic-speed walk had landed them at the door of The Cup and Chaucer.

"You know, this is almost cliché, Kenzer," said Allie, reaching for the tarnished-brass door handle. "We need to find another place to hang out. This is *Seattle!* The coffeehouse capital of America, and possibly the universe. In the U-District alone, there are twelve million coffeehouses as cool as this one."

Kenzie walked in after Allie and scoped out the café for a good table, which wasn't hard to find during the late afternoon. She lifted her backpack from her right shoulder and tossed it on the seat of a back-wall booth, sliding beside it and leaning on the table with an earnest expression on her face.

"Well...maybe. But I like The Cup. Hey, Maddy's working today—cool!

Kenzie jumped up and ran to the counter. "Maddy! What's shakin'!

"You, I figure," said Maddy, with a nod that made her dangly earrings dance. As usual, she was dressed in a funky, thrift-store ensemble—tie-dye T-shirt over a crinkly, knee-length skirt. But, Kenzie noticed, Maddy's style was becoming a bit more modest these days: no more bare midriffs. Kenzie hadn't quite figured out the quirky Maddy, whose rootless childhood had been so different from hers, but she was drawn to her free-spirited nature and zest for life.

"You've got it bad for old Chris, don't you?" kidded Maddy, putting her hand on her waist and jutting out her elbow like a diner waitress in a bad sitcom. "You didn't stay here till 1:00 A.M. the other night just to help me close the place. Good thing those seven double lattés were decaf, or you would have been buzzed for three days."

Kenzie rolled her eyes. "Okay, so it's obvious. I'm starting to 'embrace my feelings' or whatever it is y'all do on the West Coast. Hey, while you're talking, will you start me a double latté? Make it the real thing. I'm procrastinating, so I'll have to study late tonight."

Allie piped up from behind Kenzie. "I'll have a double-double half-caf cappuccino with a twist, foam on the side, please."

This time it was Maddy rolling her eyes. "If I had a dollar for every time I've heard that line…"

"You'd have just enough to rent the movie, that's all. Hardly anyone ever rents *L.A. Story*, Maddy. Steve Martin is dang funny, though, you have to admit."

"That line was funny the first ten times you said it to me, Allie. So what do you really want?" Maddy grinned and turned toward the espresso machine to start the orders, craning her neck to continue the conversation. "How about the 'Sleepless in

Seattle Special,' speaking of old movies your parents like? Four shots of espresso and a cloud of foam, with Valentine candy floating on top. I invented it myself. Cool, huh?"

"Cute. But no, thanks. You might suggest that to Ethan, though, the next time he's in here," Allie suggested. "That guy could use a good shot of caffeine. Maybe he'd actually talk. Okay, here's what I want: double café mocha with just a splash of almond syrup. Thanks, Maddy. You're the best."

In a couple of minutes, Maddy had whipped up two yummy-looking coffee creations and made change for the pals, who returned to their cozy booth.

"Finally!" said Kenzie, drowning the word in a long pull off her latté foam. "How long ago were we in the library?" Bit by bit, she filled Allie in on the rest of her dream. "So, let's hear it, Al. What do you think about my weird dream?"

Allie pulled thoughtfully at the gold hoop in her left ear. "Okay, let's start with Dylan Frost, the Flake Musician. Why do you think he was on the totem pole? Were you trying to kill him off?"

"Allie…I thought *you* were figuring this out. I don't know! But do you think that God tells us things in our dreams? Or is that too New-Agey?"

"Well, dreams are all over the Bible, you know. Remember Daniel and that guy with the funny name? Bel-something. Daniel interpreted a dream, remember? Or was that Joseph? I can't remember. Maybe we should ask Eve at Leadership on Friday," Allie suggested, referring to the Friday night meeting of college-age and adult leaders who worked with high school kids in North Seattle Young Life.

The huge crowd included the freshmen from PCU, the University of Washington, and other local colleges, who spent the first year in a concentrated spiritual-growth program, studying the Bible and books by authors such as C.S. Lewis. It was a popular group for kids who'd been involved with Young Life in high school, and many of them became Young Life leaders the following year. Kenzie, Allie, Drew and Chris had all experienced the friendship of college-age and adult leaders during high school. For Kenzie, it was her friend Gracie, a single, thirty-something career woman who cared enough to listen and share her life over late-night pizzas and Saturday morning coffee at her apartment.

Allie had friends like that, too—her high school biology teacher, Pete, and his wife Lois, who worked with Young Life in their "spare" time. Both Kenzie and Allie counted these as being among the most influential people in their lives. Now, in Seattle, they both felt close to Eve Garrett, a Young Life staffer who helped lead the Freshman Discipleship group. The Friday night meetings at the Garretts' rambling, old house had become the high point of Kenzie's week...and not just because Chris Gallagher led the singing. She was glad Allie had talked her into joining the group.

"That's a great idea," said Kenzie. "Eve'll know about dreams. Actually, if there's anybody I'd feel comfortable talking to about this, it would be her. Besides you, I mean, Al." Kenzie reached across the table and gave an affectionate tap to the bill of her friend's Stanford baseball cap.

Allie took a long sip from her café mocha. "You know, Kenzie...I think there's something you haven't told me about Dylan. You're kind of...um, elusive about him. You talked about him when we were at camp, but is there something else you want to talk about?"

Kenzie looked at her friend and laughed, much to Allie's surprise. "I can't answer that seriously. You have foam all over your nose!"

Allie touched her nose and got a handful of milky mess. *"Oh!* I thought you were going psycho on me! Okay, is that better?"* she asked, wiping the foam with a paper napkin.

"Much. Nice comic relief, though, Al. Okay. So...yeah, you're right. It's not a big deal, really. It's just that...well, Dylan and I...we sort of..." Kenzie dropped her eyes and fiddled nervously with a pack of artificial sweetener.

Allie shifted in her seat and blurted out her question: "Did you and Dylan, you know...*do* it?"

Kenzie blinked at her in surprise. "Say it, Allie—did we have sex? Well, no, thank goodness. I mean, it's not like that would have been unusual. At least half—OK, most—of the girls at Green Hills Academy did. But not me. When I was 13, Gracie talked in our small-group Bible study about sex. I just knew right then that I wanted to wait, no matter what. My mom talked about it with me, too. With three other daughters, she had the rap down by the time she got to me!"

"You're lucky, Kenz," said Allie. "My mom tried, but she couldn't pull it off. It's that old-fashioned India stuff, you know. Even though she grew up here, she couldn't quite get hip to the American ways, especially with Grandma Raju around. So I heard the talk from Lois, my Young Life leader. Anyhow...go on."

"Well, Dylan and I didn't have sex. But we came a little too close for comfort. I mean, first of all, we were kind of sneaking around anyway, because Mom and Dad just sort of tolerated him, since he was so much older, and practically unemployed, and a musician, to top it off. But he was so...you know... romantic. He'd play a song that he wrote for me, when we were off somewhere alone, in the woods or by the lake...and that just did me in."

"Define 'did me in'," said Allie, looking intently at her

friend. "I mean, not to get personal or anything, but this is obviously bothering you."

"No, not really," Kenzie hedged. "I just did things that I swore I wasn't going to do…at least till I was older, if not married."

"Hot and heavy, huh?"

"Yeah, pretty much. And it wasn't like I was totally in love with Dylan. That's what bothers me most. I knew he was…well, 'character-ally challenged.' I knew better than to get in too deep with him. But it was during my semi-rebellious, searching stage. Thank goodness I went to Malibu that summer and got my act together."

"So, was this an ongoing thing? Or just once? The hot-and-heavy stuff, I mean." Allie's look of deep concern was accentuated as she placed one hand on her chin, in a thoughtful pose.

"Two or three times, I guess," said Kenzie, swirling the remainder of her latté around in its glass. "Then I got scared, and told him we had to break up. He totally didn't understand. He gave me that 'but I love you, you're not like any other girl I've ever known' thing."

"Oldest trick in the book! Do guys think we're just totally stupid, or what?" Allie rolled her eyes in disgust.

"Well, maybe we are, sometimes, Al. But so are they!" Kenzie laughed.

"You got that right!" Allie raised her index finger for a "high-one," which Kenzie returned. "Now, tell me the rest of this. Oh, wait a minute! Kenz, are you dense? The dream, I mean! The guitar-shaped boat, the life jackets, Chris in the dorky captain's outfit, Dylan's face in the totem pole, Malibu…Hel-lo! This is totally textbook Psych 101! Don't you get it?"

Kenzie looked quizzically at Allie, who had suddenly brightened up as though she'd seen a biblical vision. "No, but apparently you do. You haven't even had Psych yet."

"I don't have to! This is so obvious, now that I think about it! Look at it, Kenz…you dreamed about Malibu, right? Your favorite place in the whole world, or one of 'em. A place where you feel totally safe and happy, right?"

"Right…"

"Okay, and you were running, right? Running to the water? Water is supposed to mean sex in dreams! Or God. I can't remember. Do you know?"

"No. That's why I asked you, you goob. Go on."

"So, you're running down to the dock, and you see Dylan's face in the totem pole. Don't you remember how, at Malibu, we used to run away from the totem poles in the dark, because they looked scary?"

"Yeah…"

"That means you're afraid of Dylan's memory, or at least of the memory of what you did. Am I right?"

"Maybe…but why is Chris in a guitar-shaped boat, in the captain's hat? And all the kids screaming, having fun in the water?"

"Hold on," said Allie. "It all falls together, I think. Hmm. Okay, at a Young Life camp, we're having fun, together, guys and girls—but it's totally wholesome, see? We're having fun, in the water, without getting into trouble! Enjoying being guys and girls, without messing around!"

"Wow," Kenzie exclaimed. "This is pretty cool, Al. You ought to be a psychologist."

"No way. They make you take math at some point. Anyway…back to your dream." Allie was getting wound up in her new role as dream analyst. "Chris, who you obviously have a crush on—and who, may I remind you, you first met at Malibu and then forgot about—Chris is inviting you onto this boat, which is a safe place to be on the water, right? And it's shaped like a guitar, which represents music, and he's wearing a captain's outfit, which means he's in charge of the boat, and concerned for its safety, and *yours*...See, Kenz? He's saying that he's safe, not like Dylan the Jerk."

"What happened to 'Dylan The Flake', Allie?" Kenzie was both engrossed and amused.

"Well, now he's a flake *and* a jerk," said Allie, impatient to get on with her explanation. "Chris is *safe*, Kenzie! He's a virgin, the Big V! Remember that cool song he wrote that he did at Leadership? 'Love Waits' I think, about waiting. And oh...I get it now! You've been using this music business thing as an excuse, haven't you? Not wanting to get close to Chris because of who your dad is. Well, pardon me for saying this, but I think you've been hiding the real reason for avoiding your feelings about Chris. Am I right? Am I right?" Allie leaned back against the back of the booth and exhaled slowly, wondering if she'd pushed too hard with her friend.

Kenzie smoothed her chestnut hair back into a temporary ponytail and let it fall back to her shoulders. Her eyes, blue as the Tennessee sky in springtime, were clouding over with emotion. "Wow. Oh, wow. Allie, are you plugged into a direct line with God, or what? This has been eating at me for a long time, and I just didn't know."

Allie smiled sweetly and reached across the table to squeeze her friend's hand. "Well, I have to admit, I've been praying about this for a while...not exactly this, but just sort of 'God, something's bugging Kenzie; help me to be a good friend.' I had no idea it was this."

Kenzie chewed her lip. "You're really a pal, Allie. I'm sorry I've been so weird about this Chris thing...and about Billy Weber, and my dad, and Emily, and everything. I feel like a jerk."

"You're not a jerk, Mary Mackenzie," said Allie, patting her friend's arm. "Just confused, that's all. And we're all far away from the people we'd usually talk to about all this kind of stuff —like Lois and Pete for me, and Gracie for you, or your Uncle What's-His-Name."

"Uncle Floyd—Dad's baby brother, the pastor. I've always been able to talk with him about almost anything. He's my buddy."

"You told your Uncle about the deal with Dylan?" Allie was astounded.

"No, not that. I should have, though. He would have under-stood. He's a great listener. And he never tells me what to do, although I usually figure it out, just by talking to him. He ought to be a psychologist, although I guess that's what makes him a great pastor."

"Wow—you have the coolest family, Kenz. My uncles are all nerds."

"Geniuses, you mean," said Kenzie, laughing. "If we could combine the Raju brains and the Dawson charm in one gene pool, we could rule the world."

"Probably so," Allie chuckled. "Now...we're not done, are we? Do we need more coffee?" she asked, digging for cash in the front pocket of her jeans.

"No...I don't want Maddy—or anybody—to see me looking like I'm about to cry."

"Hmm...maybe that's part of it, Kenz," said Allie. "Maybe you don't let people see the soft side of you. Maybe you hide the weak part with your humor and the ol' Dawson charm, hmmm?"

"Okay, that's the pot calling the kettle black!" huffed Kenzie. Her friend's puzzled expression clued Kenzie into the fact that she'd inadvertently used another Southern expression. "Which means, 'takes one to know one.' Sort of."

"Thanks for the translation, Minnie Pearl." Allie cringed. "But, *ouch!* You nailed me, sister. Yeah, okay, so I'm talking to myself, too. You and I both know it's easier to be funny than to show your weakness. So what do we do about it?"

"Allie…" Kenzie gazed pensively toward some distant corner of the room, then turned to her friend. "Allie…did you ever…you know…with a guy?"

Allie looked surprised. "I told you I hadn't, when we were bunkies at Malibu, remember?"

"Yeah, but that was almost two years ago. And you've had a boyfriend since then—Scott, right? So?"

"I'm so *sure!* Like I could get away with it, even if I wanted to! Scott was in a Young Life Bible Study with our leaders, too. With Pete and Lois staying up on our news all the time, there was no way! We would have looked too guilty. Not that I wasn't tempted, of course. Scott was a total H.O.H."

"H.O.H.?"

"'Hunk of Humanity.' So is Chris, in his own way. Kenz, you've got to get on it. That boy has got eyes for you. It's sooooo obvious."

Kenzie rolled her eyes. "Come on. We're going to miss dinner. Not that it would be a great loss." She jumped up and threw her backpack over her shoulder.

Kenzie's pace was more relaxed on the trek back to the PCU dorms. The sun had made a rare Seattle appearance that day, but it had long since gone in the two hours the girls had stayed at The Cup.

Back at the suite, Kenzie found a large note taped to the door, written in print big enough to be read easily by passersby:

KENZIE:

YOUR DAD CALLED. COMING TO SEATTLE FOR THE BOBBY OR BILL SOMEBODY SHOW NEXT MONTH. CALL HIM TONIGHT TO MAKE PLANS.

LOVE,

BETH.

Kenzie tore the note from the door and stuffed it in her pocket. Behind her, a familiar voice said, "Kenzie? Does he mean Billy Weber? Why would your dad come all the way to Seattle for that?"

It was Emily.

And Kenzie wanted to throw up.

5

Kenzie stood frozen at the door to her room, staring at Emily. "Uh, I doubt it," she stammered. "Probably something else. Hey, uh, what're they serving for dinner tonight?"

Kenzie's quick change of subject was not lost on her suitemate. Even so, Emily was hesitant to pursue the issue.

"Hamburgers or tacos. I ate early with Zoey."

Secretly, Kenzie was relieved that she wouldn't be asked to join her inquisitive roommate for dinner. Despite her moment of panic, she tried to play the friendly roommate, for Emily's benefit. "Were they good, Em? I'm starved. Allie, let's go!"

"Yeah. Pretty good…the tacos were greasy, though…" Leaving Emily looking a bit confused, Kenzie took off with Allie toward the dining hall.

"Oh, man, I am in trouble," said Kenzie. "Emily probably hates my guts, and she's really so nice. I'm a jerk."

"You're not a jerk," said Allie. "You're just stuck, that's all. You know what needs to happen, don't you?"

"I need to transfer to the University of Tennessee before next month?"

"Good grief, you're a case. No, you just come clean with Emily, that's all. With Emily, Chris, and whoever else. No big deal. No one's really going to care that your dad is president of a record company or that you are personal friends with Billy Weber. Half the people on this campus have barely heard of him, anyway—Christian music is foreign to most of the people here, you know." Allie was trying to be comforting, but it wasn't working.

"Yeah, but enough of 'em think he's the coolest to be a major problem for me. Especially You-Know-Who, with whom I happen to share a bathroom." Kenzie was practically sprinting toward the dining hall.

Allie grabbed Kenzie by the arm and twirled her around to look her in the eye.

"Kenzie, get a grip! What's the absolute worst thing that could happen? That Emily starts begging you for free CDs? That she follows you home for spring break? Or that she offers to clean your room every day for a year in exchange for Billy Weber's phone number?"

"My room's always clean anyway, except when Beth's around. And Billy's married." Kenzie frowned.

"You know what I mean. Why don't you just tell Emily and get it over with? It's not worth getting an ulcer at eighteen. Listen, I'm gonna go back to the dorm. I'm not really that hungry, and I've got to study, since we goofed around all day. I'll call ya later, 'kay?"

Allie hugged her friend and left Kenzie standing at the door of the dining hall, feeling slightly paranoid.

I guess I'm just a jerk. Maybe Allie thinks so, too.

Kenzie found a group of classmates to eat with, and carried on a light conversation as though nothing was bothering her. After a hamburger, fries, a trip to the salad bar, two Cokes and a good shot of frozen yogurt out of the machine, Kenzie took her tray back and yelled a friendly "See ya!" to her dinner companions.

On the way back to the dorm, she realized that the suite was the last place she wanted to be, after the run-in with Emily. *Wish I had my car keys,* she thought. *I'd go for a long drive somewhere. No, I wouldn't. Not in Seattle, not after dark. I'd get completely lost. I'll just go for a walk.*

Lost in thought, agonizing over her inability to act like the Christian she claimed to be, Kenzie Dawson strode around campus as if she were being followed. Eventually, she left the campus environs and within five minutes found herself on one of the busiest corners of the U-District, right in front of Baskin-Robbins. *Dessert sounds sorta good. I just had that little bit of fro-yo at dinner.*

Kenzie walked into the popular ice cream shop and began to check out the flavors listed on a bright pink sign behind the counter. *I'm in a rut,* she thought, reading names like Mango Madness and Brownie Bonanza. *I get the same thing every time…either Mint Chocolate Chip or Jamoca Almond Fudge. Boring. But awesome. I wonder whatever happened to that flavor Mom said they had when she was in high school. Mandarin Chocolate Sherbet. Sounds cool.*

Reaching in her jacket for the colorful little beaded change purse her dad had bought on a World Vision trip to Honduras, Kenzie assessed her financial situation. *Dang. Two bucks. I was going to break out of the rut and get a big ol' double-fudge brownie sundae. With Mint Chocolate Chip and Jamoca Almond Fudge.*

"Help you?" Kenzie's concentration was broken by a tall, thin man, with graying hair that was pulled into a ponytail under his brown and pink Baskin-Robbins hat. Looking up, she marveled silently at the preponderance of "old hippies" around Seattle, especially the U-District. "Oh, yeah—uh, well, I guess I'll just have a single scoop of, um…hey, do you know whatever happened to Mandarin Chocolate Sherbet?"

The man stared at her blankly for a moment. Suddenly, his face lit up as though he'd remembered a long-lost friend. "Mandarin Chocolate! Whoa, *maaaannnn!* I hadn't thought about that since I was in high school! Hey, I'll have to ask Mr. Baskin and Mr. Robbins next time I see them. Heh-heh. By the way, where are you from? That sure is a cute accent you got."

Kenzie smiled politely and put her two bills on the counter. "Thanks. I'm from Tennessee. Umm, I'd like a scoop of Mint Chocolate Chip on a—"

"Hey, KENZIE! What, the ice cream at school isn't good enough for ya?" Kenzie turned around and saw Drew, Ethan, and Ryan coming in the front door. "Oh, hi, guys!"

"What're you havin', Kenz? I'm buyin', go for it!" Drew was always ready to treat—but Kenzie felt it was the act of a truly generous heart, not a rich, insecure guy trying to buy friendship.

"Well, Drew, tell you what—you can spot me a couple of bucks for what I really wanted. I'll pay you back."

"No way! Give the lady what she wants, pal," Drew tossed a twenty on the counter and gestured to the old hippie scoop-jockey.

"Okay," Kenzie relented. "Make that a double-fudge brownie sundae—one scoop each of Mint Chocolate Chip and Jamoca Almond Fudge," she said, a tad sheepishly. "These guys'll help me eat it."

The chocolatey treat didn't last long after Kenzie brought it to the table. Even though the three guys had ample ice cream of their own, Kenzie had to fight to keep invading spoons out of her bowl.

"Hey, guys, if you hadn't shown up, I'd be eating peacefully by myself," she joked. "But go ahead. Especially you, Drew."

"Hey, Kenzie, don't you wish we'd brought Chris with us?" Ryan was using his role as Cooper's boyfriend to become the suite's official Annoying Big Brother, a role he'd already well established with Emily.

Kenzie "batted her eyes just right," as her dear "Grandmimi" Chalmers used to say, in a Southern fashion that would have made her grandmother proud. Then she laid on the Scarlett O'Hara accent, thick and syrupy: "Why, Ryan! Why would I need any othah gentlemen heah when ah've got all of you fine strappin' gentlemen?"

Ryan looked only semi-convinced.

"Whatever. Anyway, he's meeting us here in a minute. We went to the *Robo-Cop III* matinee without him—he was working on a song or something. Might play it tonight at The Cup," he said. Ryan winked at her, in fine big-brother style, and dug at the brownie in Kenzie's dish. Then he proceeded to give her all the details of that afternoon's movie, which he had obviously enjoyed.

A minute later, Chris walked in the door, toting his guitar. "Sorry I missed the movie, guys, but I finished the song—Oh! Uh…hi, Kenzie!" His face lit up when he noticed her, surrounded by his buddies.

"Hi, Chris." She smiled, glad he'd made it. *I can't explain how I feel about him—it's not the usual crush. I feel like I could be his best friend. And kiss him, too…* "I heard you missed *Robo-Cop III*. What a tragedy. Such a fine film."

"It's a guy thing," he said, focusing his attention on her laughing blue eyes. "Your brother's seen it, I'm sure."

"If I had a brother, I'm sure he would have. In my family, it's *Little Women* all the way. We've got four girls. We got together at the theater and got all mushy." She grinned right at Chris, feeling comfortable and happy to be talking with him.

"It wasn't bad for a chick flick," Ryan interjected. "My sister made me go see it with her. Bummer about that one sister who croaks, though. Emmie sobbed through that part."

Chris slipped his guitar off his shoulder and sat on a pink plastic chair.

"I saw it, too, Kenzie," he said, not paying attention to Ryan. "With my mom. I liked it a lot." He cleared his throat and affected a deep voice. "I mean…yeah, for a chick flick, it wasn't bad." He laughed, as though he'd been caught in a less-than-manly confession. Kenzie took a mental note. *He liked* Little Women? *It takes a real man to admit that…*

"Maybe we could see it sometime if it comes back around. Or rent it."

Kenzie looked around, unsure if he was talking to her, or the guys.

"I think he means you, Kenzie. I'm not watchin' it again." Ryan shook his head and smiled. "*Terminator 2,* well, that's another thing. I'm all over that, Chris. Right, guys?" He looked around for affirmation.

"Right," agreed Drew.

"Sure," said Ethan.

"Yeah, Chris, you and Kenzie go right ahead and watch *Little Women.* We'll let you get away with it, since you're the sensitive musician."

Chris smiled and shook his head, folded his arms across his chest, then stuck his hand out for Ryan to slap. "Okay, Stewart, I'll watch *Terminator 2* with you. Maybe I'll write a song about Schwarzenegger."

"Cool! Knew we could count on ya, buddy."

"Well, listen…I hate to not eat and run. I know I promised to stop by, but I'm running late and I've still got to go set up at

The Cup. Hope you guys'll come by later." Chris looked right at Kenzie as he issued the invitation.

"We'll be there. I will, anyway." Kenzie surprised herself at how bold she was acting, right in front of her guy friends. *Might as well.*

Kenzie got up and walked Chris to the door, then out to the sidewalk.

"Are you going to be at Leadership this Friday?" Chris asked hopefully.

Kenzie looked down and picked at the cuff of her dusty-green leather jacket. "Wouldn't miss it. You?" She raised her head and peered into Chris's eyes.

"I wouldn't miss it, either. Besides, they'd kill me if I didn't show up. For such a big group, they're pretty short on guitar players in North Seattle Young Life. Anyway, I might…"

"Might what?" Kenzie looked at him quizzically.

"Might do a new song. A worship song. Not the one I just wrote tonight. That's kind of a…a love song. More Cup style. Hope you, uh…can come by later." Chris started pulling at his own sleeve, and shifted the weight of the guitar on his shoulder.

"I've gotta study, but…I'll probably need a break later." Kenzie pulled her jacket tighter around her. "Brrrr…it's cold, isn't it?" But she knew it was not the weather, but the feeling of falling for somebody that made her shiver.

"You better go inside. See you later, I hope." Chris opened the door to Baskin-Robbins and waited till Kenzie was inside before he waved and walked away.

Inside, the guys were still discussing *Robo-Cop III,* but when Kenzie walked in, Ryan made mention of her brief absence.

"You and Chris were, uh, kind of into each other. You goin' to The Cup, then?" He raised his eyebrows.

"Well, maybe. I have to study, though." Kenzie walked

behind each of the guys and rubbed their shoulders for a minute, dispensing friendly flirtations.

"What a night! Y'all are just the best! Three of the hottest catches at PCU, and I'm on a date with all of 'em! Am I lucky, or what? Well, I'm walking back to school. Thanks, guys—"

As she turned to leave, Ryan reached out and tugged at her sleeve. "Hey, I've got my truck. Why don't you come back with us? Southern gentlemen wouldn't let a lady walk home alone, would they?"

Kenzie gave them all a playfully shy, Scarlett-like smile and relented. Soon, she was riding shotgun in the cab with Ryan, while Ethan and Drew rode in the back, in the open truck bed.

Ryan turned down the tape that was blasting on the stereo.

"Hey, Kenzie, can I ask you about something? I've noticed that Emily has been acting kinda weird the last couple of weeks, like somebody hurt her feelings or something. And she won't talk to me about it."

Oh, no, thought Kenzie. *I walked all the way here to get away from this, and now it's in my face.*

"Would you talk to Emmie?" Ryan asked. "She's had a hard enough time, with her best friend not coming to school and rooming with her, you know. And then she's been getting over that John guy. That was a major blow. Maybe that's all there is to it. But could you find out if something else is going on? She's kind of cut me out of the loop lately. Guess it's weird for her to see me and Cooper together, too, huh?"

Kenzie glanced at Ryan and found herself wishing she had a brother like him.

"Em and I aren't really super close, Ryan. We sort of hang around different people. I mean, she's really great...so nice. A great suite-mate, really..."

Kenzie wondered if her discomfort was obvious enough for

Ryan to catch on that Emily's problem just *might* be Kenzie. But he didn't pick up on that, much to her relief.

"Well, I'd appreciate it if you'd talk to her," Ryan said, popping the tape out of the deck. "She really respects you. She says you're the coolest suite-mate of them all. Sometimes I think she wishes that I was dating you instead of Cooper! No chance! I mean, I'd have to duke it out with Chris for you, anyway…hey, do you know who Billy Weber is? I have his new tape here and it's pretty cool. Wanna listen to this one song real quick?"

The truck had pulled up in front of Kenzie's dorm, and Ryan let the engine idle. "Uh, no, thanks," said Kenzie, opening the door and sliding out onto the sidewalk. "I think Emily's been playing the CD around the suite."

"Oh, yeah! Sure. Hey, I hear he's coming to town. I'm sure Emily will want to go—she's his biggest fan in the world. Did she tell you about the time she mailed homemade chocolate chip cookies to his record company? I told her he'd never get 'em, but she did it anyway. Kinda dumb, I know, but she's nuts about him. If she wasn't my own sister, I'd think she had 'wacko fan' tendencies. I mean, I like his music too, but I'm not gonna send him cookies. Anyhow, we should get a block of tickets and all go together. If you like him, that is."

Kenzie had that Unfortunate Vomiting Incident feeling creeping up on her. "Sure, yeah, that would be great. Okay, gotta go. I'll talk to Em.

"Bye, guys!" she shouted to Drew and Ethan. "Thanks for helping me eat all that ice cream. Couldn't have done it without y'all!"

She waved them off and sprinted to the door of the dorm, wondering if her knotted stomach would hold down a hamburger, fries, salad, two Cokes, frozen yogurt and one-fourth of a double-fudge brownie sundae with a scoop each of Mint

Chocolate Chip and Jamoca Almond Fudge. She took the stairs instead of the elevator, just in case.

When she arrived at the suite, Billy Weber's new CD was blasting in the living room. Beth was nowhere to be found, as usual, and Cooper's oversized NEW YORK CITY TRANSIT AUTHORITY keychain was not on the goofy wooden SOUVENIR OF GREAT SMOKY MOUNTAINS combination key-hook and mail catcher that Kenzie had brought from Tennessee. Despite Cooper's tendency to completely mess up her room, she usually managed to keep her keys on the hook.

Uh-oh, thought Kenzie. *Billy's on the CD player, Coop and Beth aren't home...Emily's in her room, guaranteed.*

Suddenly, Kenzie remembered that the previous Sunday, her pastor had spoken about integrity in relationships. When he'd cited the verse about "speaking the truth in love," she'd felt a deep conviction to start being honest about things with Emily, Chris, and others. Unfortunately, that feeling of conviction hadn't moved her to action.

Not yet, anyway. *Help me, Lord. I can't do this, but I know I need to...just give me the words...*

She saw light coming from under the door of Emily and Cooper's bedroom. *Here goes...*

Kenzie put her ear against the door to listen for sounds. Suddenly, the door opened and she fell, off balance, into the room, against a startled Emily.

"Oh, gosh, I'm sorry! I was just—" Kenzie was mortified to think Emily suspected her of spying.

"I...I was just going to turn off the stereo," stammered Emily, clutching a plaid-covered notebook that Kenzie assumed was a journal. "I was just going to have a little quiet time, since no one was here."

That admission made Kenzie feel even worse, considering

that she hadn't cracked her Bible since Sunday morning at church.

"Well, maybe we should talk," mumbled Kenzie.

"What?" said Emily, a little incredulously.

"I mean, I need to explain a few things. I know I haven't been very, well—nice lately. I've been sort of a jerk, really…um, do you want some Red Zinger tea?"

Emily looked at Kenzie as if she had just sprouted an extra head.

"Tea? No, thanks, I have a Diet Coke here, do you want some?"

"No, no." Kenzie decided it was time to quit stalling. "Okay. So, um, Em…Ryan's worried about you. He thinks you're having a hard time, and—" *C'mon, Kenz…be straight with her.* "Em, I think I know what's wrong with you. I've been a jerk, I know. It's just that…well, how do I explain this?"

Emily, being kind, tried hard to relieve Kenzie's discomfort, even if it was at her own expense. "It's okay, Kenzie. Part of it is just that I really do miss my friend Holly," she said, referring to the friend from home who had been her first choice for a room-mate. "We had made so many plans for PCU. It was hard when she had to stay home…I mean, Cooper's great, but it's so weird that she's dating my brother! He's always over here, and I really wanted to be on my own…I mean, with Holly. And this city is so big, and my classes are so hard compared to high school, and I miss my mom and dad, and my church group, and—"

Kenzie couldn't take it anymore. "EM! STOP IT!" She yelled loud enough for Emily to widen her eyes in shock. Kenzie looked at the wall, then at Emily. "I know why you've been acting weird lately, and it's me. I've been a jerk. Like at the post office, when I've gotten those packages, you know?"

"Well, yes, I've wondered why you've been so mysterious

about that." Emily sat down on her bed and took a sip from her drink.

Kenzie looked around the room. Cooper's side was a wreck, as usual, with clothes draped over every available piece of furniture and various cosmetic items, books and coins strewn all over the dresser. Emily's side was in perfect order, down to the neat, organized desk next to her bed, with its snugly tucked dark green and blue bedcovers and complementary plaid pillow shams. It was a sight for Kenzie's sore eyes—her roommate Beth could trash the room in fifteen minutes, which was about all the time she ever spent there.

Maybe Em and I have more in common than I thought, mused Kenzie to herself. *This could be my room, easy, with the softball trophy on the shelf and the Nike posters…Although the Billy Weber shrine is a bit much…*

"Em, do you like Billy Weber?" Kenzie couldn't believe what she heard herself saying.

"Of course; he's the coolest! Don't you?" Emily lit up at the mention of his name, which made Kenzie cringe inside. Still, the words of last Sunday's sermon kept coming back: *Speaking the truth in love…*

"Yeah, me too. He's great, huh? Anyhow, maybe we could all go to the show together. I'll let you know."

Suddenly, Kenzie realized there was no way she could tell Em the truth. Not then. It was just too much. She needed more time. *God will understand.*

"That would be so fun!" Emily seemed like a new woman. Maybe it was enough that Kenzie was paying attention to her.

"I'm sorry I've been so distant lately," said Kenzie, weaseling her way out of the truth. "I've been too wrapped up in my own stuff to be a good roomie." *Which is true…*

"Like trying so hard not to fall for Chris?" Emily was smiling, like an adoring little sister.

Oh, brother, thought Kenzie. *But at least she thinks it's something else...geez, I'm a jerk!*

"Yeah. I guess it's no secret anymore, huh?" Kenzie managed a weak laugh and stood up. "Well, I have to study. I goofed around all afternoon and I have a history test tomorrow. Fortunately, it's on the Civil War, and we know all about that in the South, you know. The Wawuh Between The States. The Great Nawthun Aggression. The Late Unpleasantness."

Once again, Kenzie was using humor to deflect discomfort. In this case, the discomfort was her own. But Emily loved it.

"You are *so* funny! I wish I were as funny as you. To tell you the truth, as much as I like Cooper, I was kind of hoping that you and Ryan would—"

Kenzie interrupted her confession. "No way! Ry and Coop are great together! Besides, you just said I had a thing for Chris, didn't you? Guess you nailed it, Em! We'll see if he ever asks me out, though."

"Oh, Chris is sooo cute! And so talented! I'll bet *he's* going to see Billy Weber next month! Don't you think Chris is good enough to make records one day? Hey, maybe you guys'll get married, and then he'd dedicate his albums to you? Wouldn't that be totally romantic?"

Emily was really pushing it now. Kenzie's stomach was reminding her of the greasy fries she'd consumed at the dining hall.

"Em...he barely knows I'm alive—hey, listen, I'm going to study, okay? I'll see you later."

"Thanks for the talk, Kenzie," said Emily, beaming. "I feel a lot better now. You know, I'm really glad we're suite-mates. It helps me not to miss Holly so much. I think you and I are gonna be great friends. I hope so, anyway," she added shyly.

Kenzie nodded as pleasantly as she could manage, went to her room, and closed the door. Without pausing, she let herself fall face down onto the bed.

"I'm a jerk," she moaned into her pillow. "A bonafide, first-class, cold-hearted jerk."

Take a hike, Kenzie.

It wasn't really a voice, but the idea came to Kenzie as clear as if it had been spoken. Take a hike? That was a terrible thing to say, but she figured she deserved it, if it was the voice of her conscience.

Take a hike, Kenzie.

This time, she got it. *Oh! Take a hike! As in, a walk in the mountains!*

That's it. Time with God, alone, where she could express her frustrations, pray, cry, yell if she needed to—like she had always done on the ridgetop at Radnor Lake at home, or in the Smoky Mountains, at her family's cabin. *Time with God. That's what I need.*

Hmmm. Maybe it was his idea...

6

The next morning, Kenzie woke up raring to go. The thought of getting away to commune with nature and God made her happier than she'd been in weeks. She whistled in the shower, while she dressed and packed her backpack for class, and even while she walked to the dining hall with Beth, who had shown up late the night before for a rare sleepover in the room. She'd come in long after Kenzie was asleep, but woke up to Kenzie's 8:00 alarm and decided to join her for coffee.

"How can you whistle this early in the morning?" groaned Beth, bleary-eyed and barely awake. "And how do you know how to, anyway?"

Kenzie stopped whistling. "I don't even know I'm doing it, half the time. My dad is a great whistler. Did you know only one out of ten women can whistle? At least, that's what I heard."

"From who?" asked Beth, brushing her hair as the two walked across the lawn to the dining hall. "I mean, 'whom'? Is it who or whom? I can never remember. I think I got it wrong on the SAT."

"It's…well, never mind," said Kenzie. "It's too early to worry about being grammatically correct. Wait till you've had some coffee, anyway."

As Kenzie chatted away, she thought about how easy it was to get along with Beth, who was rarely around the suite, and how hard it was to be around the ever-present Emily—for no good reason, except Kenzie's own fear.

Kenzie considered asking Beth about her boyfriend, but she didn't want to make waves—even though the two were so obviously spending the nights together, and had been since the beginning of fall semester.

I think she's a Christian, thought Kenzie. *She's got a Bible in the nightstand by her bed, but she's hardly ever in her bed. I wonder if she feels guilty. I'm not going to ask her, though.*

The dining hall was typically busy for 8:30, so Kenzie and Beth had to stand in line for a crack at the breakfast line.

"I'm not really hungry," said Beth. "I'll just grab some coffee and find us a table, OK, Kenzie? Just you and me, if you don't mind."

"Sure, that's great." Kenzie was a tad bewildered at Beth's sudden interest in having a roomie-only breakfast. Bewildered and a bit nervous. *Please, God. I'm having enough trouble with Emily. Don't tell me Beth's ticked off at me, too! I can't wait to get out of here and go hike a mountain.*

Kenzie loaded up a tray with pancakes, bacon, two bananas, a tall glass of O.J., and a cup of coffee, heavy on the cream. Fending off various invitations to join a loud, boisterous group of friends at a big table near the front of the dining hall, Kenzie walked to the back of the room to join Beth at a corner two-seater.

"Gross! How in the world can you eat all that stuff in the morning?" Beth gave Kenzie's abundant breakfast a look of disgust with her red-rimmed eyes. "I can do coffee and a bagel or a muffin—that's it. And that's on a good day. Besides, how can you eat like that and not get fat? I just look at a pancake and gain half a pound."

"I shoot hoops," Kenzie said, lathering her pancakes with butter.

"What?" said Beth, obviously confused.

"Basketball. I play basketball—for fun, now, but I played on my high school team. I run, too, and hike and stuff. In fact, I'm going hiking today after my morning classes." Kenzie reached for the syrup pitcher and poured a graceful, cascading stream over her towering pancake stack.

"Cool!" said Beth, in the most enthusiastic voice she'd used that morning.

Kenzie wondered if her roommate's new-found energy was caffeine-induced. *Maybe she really does like hiking. Or the way I poured the syrup.* "Could I go with you? I haven't really done anything like that since I've been here."

"Uh, well, I…" Kenzie looked down and carved a wedge of pancakes from the perfectly aligned stack. Dredging it through a pool of syrup, she poised the bite near her mouth and wondered how to tell Beth that she needed to be alone.

Beth continued. "It's just that I…I know I haven't been much of a roommate, and I thought maybe we could get to know each other better, and…" She hesitated, picking up on Kenzie's lack of excitement about the idea, but pushed on. "Okay, it's more like…well, I really need to talk to somebody, and I haven't really made any friends since I've been at PCU, except for my boyfriend, and—Forget it, I shouldn't barge in on your plans."

Kenzie took her pancake bite and practically swallowed it whole, washing it down with a big swig of juice. She looked at Beth and wondered if that was a tear forming in the corner of her eye.

"Do you want to talk about something, Beth?" Kenzie surprised herself with the compassion she heard in her own voice.

"I sort of need to get away by myself in the mountains today, but maybe we could have a latté or something when I get back. Maybe after dinner?" Kenzie was also a little surprised at her own honesty about needing to be alone. *I must really need this,* she thought.

"It's no big deal," said Beth. "It's not like I'm pregnant or anything." Kenzie sighed inwardly in secret relief. "It's just that...for some reason, I'm starting to wonder if what I'm doing is right. Do you know what I mean?" Beth rubbed the edge of her coffee cup with her thumbs and looked up at Kenzie. *Those are tears.*

"You mean sleeping with Brad?" Once again, Kenzie couldn't believe what was coming out of her own mouth.

"Yes..." Beth's tears were now falling slowly down her face. Kenzie grabbed a handful of napkins from the table dispenser and offered them to her roommate, trying hard to avoid checking her watch as she did it. *I'm going to be late for class, but this is important. God, help me.*

"Kenzie...I hardly even know you, but I know you're a Christian, and I am too. I just haven't been a good one. Listen, I know you have a nine o'clock class...we can talk about this later. Really. I don't want to make you late. You're just so nice, and I thought maybe you would understand...I just don't know who to talk to...Cooper's gone a lot, and Emily's around, but I just don't relate to her very well. She's just such a good Christian...oh, I mean, not that you're not..."

Kenzie touched Beth's arm in a reassuring gesture. "I know what you mean. Believe me, I take that as a compliment," she said, with a gentle laugh. "I'm not perfect, if that's what you're trying to say. Emily seems almost too good to be true, right?"

"That's it, exactly," said Beth, mopping her eyes with a sodden napkin. "You just seem like you've...well, like you've experienced more than Emily has. No offense or anything."

"Hey, I know. Em's a great girl. She's just led kind of a sheltered life, that's all. I guess having a big brother like Ryan protected her from stuff. My sisters never threatened to beat up my boyfriends."

Beth laughed, and blew her nose on a dry napkin. She looked thankful for the comic relief. "You're so cool, Kenzie. Thanks for listening to me…we can talk later, OK? Don't be late for class."

"I'd better not; I have a test," said Kenzie, suddenly remembering the Civil War exam. She stuffed the two bananas in her backpack for brain fuel, put on her jacket, and reached down to pick up her tray of barely touched pancakes.

"I'll bus your tray," said Beth. "It's the least I can do for hogging your breakfast time."

"Thanks, but you didn't hog anything. I'm glad we talked. See you back at the suite later?"

"Yeah. Good luck on your exam. And have a great time hiking, okay? Say a prayer for me, if you don't mind."

"You got it. I'd be glad to," said Kenzie, stifling a strange urge to hug the girl that she'd referred to since September as "The Phantom."

I could use some prayer myself, thought Kenzie, picking up her pace on the way to History 110—United States since 1860. *Especially for this exam—Dr. Sullivan may be a cool prof, but he's no cream puff.*

To her great relief, Kenzie discovered she had written the wrong date in her class planner—the exam was scheduled for the next week. Grateful for the reprieve, she paid close attention to the lecture and made careful notes as the young, cute Dr. Sullivan lectured on the economic impact of slavery in the agricultural economy in the nineteenth century South. It wasn't until he was wrapping up the political implications of the Kansas-Nebraska Act of 1854 that Kenzie's mind took her to a mountain trail overlooking Puget Sound.

"For next time, read chapters 5 and 6 in the Wilson text, and the second selection from Owenby. And don't forget: exam next Wednesday. Sally forth, troops. Be strong and courageous."

The prof's standard, quaint end-of-class charge woke Kenzie from her reverie. She wondered how many other students knew that the last part was a direct quote from the Bible—although she couldn't remember from which book or who said it. *Joshua, I think…or Moses. I'll look it up on my hike, maybe.*

For the second great surprise of the day, Kenzie found a note attached to the door of Eng 222—American Lit, Dr. RoseAnne Coleman: CLASS CANCELLED DUE TO ILLNESS. READ FAULKNER, WELTY AND HANNAH SHORT STORIES FROM ANTHOLOGY FOR NEXT TIME. YES, THERE WILL BE A QUIZ ON THE READINGS. - DR. COLEMAN

Kenzie grinned at Allie, who was also in the class. "Cool! I'm outta here!" As Allie headed toward the library, Kenzie ran to her dorm and dumped her books out of her backpack. In their place, she threw in her journal and a pocket Bible. Next, she grabbed her hiking boots, extra socks, some cash, bottled water, and the keys to her faithful Jeep. Within minutes, she was off campus and heading out of the city—but not before driving through Wendy's for a chicken club sandwich with onions, fries and a big Coke, which she devoured in the half hour it took her to reach Mount Si, just outside of the quaint little town of Snoqualmie.

Wow! Kenzie sat in the car, lacing up her hiking boots and gazing out of the window at a spectacular view of the Cascade Mountains. *This is so unbelievably cool. I can't believe I haven't hiked up here a million times already! I've gotta thank Drew for*

telling me about this. Although I'll bet Chris told him about it first.

After a quick pit stop at the park facilities, Kenzie shouldered her pack and started up the trail, absentmindedly whistling a Billy Weber tune. *Listen to me,* she thought, after she realized what she was whistling. *I can't get away from it! Oh, God, help me…I feel like such a hypocrite. I practically lied to my roommate, I've taken my sweet time being friendly to a great guy that I actually like a lot, I'm totally disloyal to my dad, our family friends.*

The more Kenzie thought about the way she had acted since coming to PCU, the faster she walked, hardly noticing the flora and fauna. In truth, Kenzie Dawson, the PCU forestry major, couldn't name more than three trees native to the Pacific Northwest.

Some grateful child I am. Christian music—especially Billy Weber's music—has pretty much paid my way through life, and I come to Seattle to get away from it. Then I have to act like I've never heard of it, or LightSong Records, or Billy…I'm just a jerk. Besides that, I come up here to be selfish instead of inviting my poor roommate Beth, who's all torn up about sleeping with her boyfriend. At least I think that's what she was talking about. What kind of Christian am I, anyway?

By now, the grade of the Mount Si slope had increased considerably, and Kenzie found herself huffing, puffing and sweating, despite her excellent physical condition. "Holy cow! These are serious mountains," she said aloud, to no one in particular. *Oh, yeah,* she remembered. *They're higher than the Smokies, and more dramatic, because they're younger. The Smokies are more rounded, glaciated—part of the Appalachian Range, the oldest in America.* Kenzie pulled those "Fun Facts" from some mental file on mountain ranges, and was rather impressed with herself for a brief moment.

These mountains are spectacular because they're young, not
mature like the Smokies, which have a beauty and majesty all their
own. The Smokies never try to deny who they are.

"You are *so* weird," Kenzie said to herself. Whenever she was
alone in the mountains, Kenzie eventually started voicing her
thoughts out loud. "As *if* Smokies could think about their place
in the world! Get a grip!"

At that point, Kenzie needed to get a grip on more than just
her thoughts. She had hiked hard and fast up a very steep trail.
As a result, her head was throbbing and she was starting to feel
woozy.

She slowed down her pace and walked for awhile until she
found an inviting wide spot on the trail, where she plopped
down for a rest. Through the fir trees, she could see a rare
glimpse of the astonishingly beautiful Mount Rainier, which
was usually blocked by Seattle's world-famous rain clouds. On
this bright winter afternoon, however, the skies were clear, and
Kenzie could soak up the scene—the shining white peak,
jagged and dramatic against a cobalt blue sky.

Wouldn't Mom have a cow if she knew I was up here all by
myself, in the mountains? Kenzie thought for a moment. *No, she*
wouldn't. She knows.

Long ago, Kenzie and her mom had come to an understanding about Kenzie's hikes. Kenzie used to hike up to the
Ganier Ridge all the time, at Radnor Lake, a state nature reserve
on the outskirts of Nashville, not far from the Dawsons' house.
Ganier Ridge was the place Kenzie went when she needed to
hike off her problems. Playing basketball helped. So did running. But hiking to the top of the ridge, hearing the wind
through the trees, was for Kenzie a source of peace like no
other.

And Kenzie's mom never worried about her there, or so

Kenzie believed. She never asked, either—she just seemed to understand when Kenzie had to bolt out of the house, in sock feet, carrying her Nike Hikers over her shoulder, by their strings.

This could be my Ganier Ridge, Kenzie thought. *Seattle version.*

Pulling out her journal, a black Stabilo Sensor pen, and her pocket Bible, Kenzie leaned against a massive pine tree and sighed deeply, feeling wonderfully tingly from the strenuous hike and exhausted from the conflict in her soul.

"I wish Uncle Floyd was here!" In her frustration, Kenzie spoke out loud. "He'd understand. Okay, Lord. I know. You're here."

Kenzie flipped the pages of her little Bible to the Psalms, a book that never failed to give her some peace and perspective. Rather than reading from her modern translation, however, she spoke the first line of Psalm 121 from memory. As the words from her old King James Version rose to her lips, Kenzie felt as though she were Granny Dawson herself, rocking on the front porch of her Smoky Mountain cabin, Bible in her lap: "I will lift up mine eyes unto the hills, from whence cometh my help."

Granny, who was actually Kenzie's great-grandmother, had lived to be ninety-five years old, and couldn't see much of anything in her last years. It didn't matter, though, when it came to the Bible. Granny would keep it in her lap and recite favorite verses from memory for all who visited.

The verse about the mountains was usually misinterpreted, she explained to Kenzie and her sisters in her sweet, East Tennessee mountain drawl. "It's not a statement, don't you know. 'From whence cometh my help' is a question, answered in the next sentence: 'My help cometh even from the Lord, which made heaven and earth.' The psalmist knew his trust was in the creator of those hills. And I know it, too. Like him, I look to these mountains when I pray, and God always gives me what I need. You'uns do the same, children."

Kenzie looked up from her Bible toward Mount Rainier, but the view was blurred by tears. "Oh, Lord…forgive me." Kenzie prayed through wet sniffles, confident that she was being heard. "I've been so worried about what people think about me. You gave me the greatest family and friends back home who love me, no matter what I do or how I act…and here I am trying to get away and make a new life for myself with new friends, and for what? So I can be 'just Kenzie Dawson,' without a history, all by myself? I've been the biggest phony of them all, and I hate phonies more than anything. I'm so sorry. Please help me to be honest. I can't do this without your strength."

She cried for a long time, letting the tears flow unhindered. Then, one of Granny Dawson's famous sayings popped into her head. Kenzie laughed out loud, through her tears, as she remembered what Granny had said to Kenzie's dad, right by the grave at Great-Granddad's funeral: "Those tears have been a long time coming, haven't they, child? That's all right. You go ahead. The more you cry, the less you pee."

"I have the best family in the world," Kenzie said, laughing and crying at the same time. "And a great history—a treasure. Oh, Lord, I'm such a fool for trying to be somebody I'm not. Thank you for using Your word to show me that."

And Granny Dawson, too, Kenzie thought. She stood up, wiped her face on the sleeve of her sweatshirt, and practically skipped down the trail, whistling "Just A Closer Walk With Thee," a favorite old hymn of Granny's which The Little Dawson Brothers once played on the stage of the Grand Ole Opry.

Somehow, I think Granny knows. Thanks, Lord.

7

By the time Kenzie got back to campus, clouds had moved in and blocked the view of Mount Rainier, but the clouds around her heart were long gone. Grinning, she pulled her Jeep into a spot in the dorm parking lot and ran all the way to her suite, where she planned to change into workout clothes to shoot baskets down at the gym.

Just before she reached the suite door, however, she remembered that she'd promised to find Beth for a latté and a talk. By now, Kenzie figured, Beth was probably an emotional wreck, waiting to spill her guts.

"Oh, hey, Kenzie! How was your hike? You look like you had a great one! Great weather for the mountains, huh?" Beth was not only at the suite, she was alarmingly cheerful for someone who'd been weeping in the dining hall just that morning.

"Yeah, it was great. I had a great time." Kenzie tried to assess Beth's mood. "Maybe we could go together sometime. Hey, did you want to go get a latté or something? We said we were going to do that, right?" She looked quizzically at Beth, who was actually folding her clothes and putting them in the dresser drawers, something Kenzie had never seen her do before.

"Oh, no, that's okay. Brad and I are going to the movie at the Union after dinner, with Ryan and Cooper. Thanks anyway, though! Maybe another time." Beth acted as if their conversation that morning had never taken place. "Oh, by the way, your dad called. Said you *need* to call him to make plans for his trip out here. Isn't that what he said, Em?" Beth yelled the last part around the corner.

"What? Oh, yeah, Kenzie, your dad wants you to call him about something," Emily said, as she trotted into Kenzie and Beth's room.

What is the deal here, God? Kenzie sighed. *Suddenly, Beth is OK and is big pals with Cooper and Ryan? And Emily talked to my dad?*

"It was actually a woman who called," said Emily, as if she were reading Kenzie's mind. "Your dad's secretary or assistant or something. She said you should call him at the office to plan for his trip out here."

"That's what Beth said," Kenzie muttered, feeling her buoyant spirits drop. "I'll call him. Are you sure that's all she said? By the way, that was Martha, and she's a vice president, not his secretary. I mean, she used to be his secretary...never mind."

"Yes, that was it. She said you'd know what she meant."

Kenzie nodded, feeling angry that she had lost her resolve to be honest. *It hasn't even been an hour since I was up on the mountain. Why can't I do the right thing?*

"Hey, would y'all mind moving to the living room for a minute? I need to call my dad." Kenzie gave Beth and Emily each a friendly shove on the shoulder.

"Sure, Kenzie," Emily chirped. "Oh! I almost forgot to ask— if we don't get tickets soon, the Billy Weber concert will be sold out. Do you want to go? I need to know, so I can get all our seats together."

Oh no, thought Kenzie. *I just can't tell her the truth. I am a complete and total loser.*

"Uh, let me think about it," Kenzie said brusquely. "After I call my dad, maybe. I'll let you know."

"What*ev*-er." Emily had never used that tone before, that Kenzie could remember. *Poor Em. She didn't know she was getting a schizoid for a suite-mate.*

Kenzie shut the door, dialed the phone, and fell back on her neatly made bed. After two rings, she heard a recorded voice saying "Thank you for calling The LightSong Corporation. Our offices are open Monday through Friday, from 9 to 6 Central Time—"

Glancing at her watch, Kenzie realized that it was just after six back in Nashville. She punched in the extension number for her dad's private line, certain that he'd still be around somewhere, since Martha had asked her to call him there.

A mature-sounding woman with a soft, musical Southern accent answered immediately: "Johnny Dawson's office."

"Martha? It's Kenzie! What are you doing answering the old man's phone? You're a dang vice president now!"

"Well, Mary Mackenzie! Isn't this a treat? I just happened to be walking by and picked it up out of habit, I guess. You cute thing, what in the world are you doing out there? When are you moving back? We hate it that you're not around here anymore. Are you staying out of trouble? Starting some is more like it, knowing you!"

Kenzie stretched her legs up against her bedroom wall and stared at her hiking boots, imagining Martha Rosewood's rust-red hair and full-of-fun green eyes. She had known Martha all her life and thought of her as a favorite aunt, not just a long-time employee of LightSong. Martha had been good friends with Kenzie's mother since grade school. In fact, it was Martha who had introduced Johnny Dawson and Peggy Chalmers.

"No, ma'am, I haven't been picked up by the campus police yet. But it's only the end of January. Plenty of time left in the semester."

"Your dad was probably calling about the trip to Seattle, for Billy's show," said Martha. "Are any of your friends going?"

"Funny you should ask. My suite-mate was just trying to get me to commit to it. Tickets are going fast." In frustration, Kenzie gave a slight kick to her bedroom wall.

"So you still haven't let the cat out of the bag, have you, honey?" Martha's question contained not a hint of accusation.

"Martha, thank you for understanding about this," Kenzie said gratefully. "I wish I could explain it to Mom and Dad, but it would really hurt their feelings. Especially Dad."

"Kenzie Dawson, I don't think you give those parents of yours near enough credit. You're the fourth child they've raised, don't forget. They pick up on a lot more than you think. Especially with you. You're not that good about hiding your feelings, you know. Besides, don't you think Johnny Dawson will be suspicious if you don't ask for concert passes for your friends?"

Kenzie squirmed. "Yeah, you're right. The thing is, I thought I'd figured this all out today. I went hiking and everything. I even prayed about it. But now I feel confused all over again."

"Now listen, dear girl—you just be yourself and don't worry about it. Enjoy being with your daddy and Billy. You're proud of them, aren't you?"

"Yes, ma'am," said Kenzie, with quiet hesitation. "It's just that— "

"I know, honey, I know. You wanted to get away from all of this, didn't you? And now it's following you all the way to Seattle."

Kenzie's eyes welled up with tears that rolled down the sides of her cheeks, over her collar, and onto the bed.

"Kenzie? Honey, are you all right?" Hearing a voice as familiar and beloved as Martha's made the tears fall even faster.

"I'm okay," Kenzie sniffled. "It's just that I've been such a phony. Why am I crying about this? I thought I'd worked it all out—"

"You can't expect it to be fixed right away, honey. Life's still here when you come down from the mountaintop, isn't it? One thing at a time, sweet girl. You're awfully hard on yourself, you know. You always have been." Martha's words were clear and true, and comforting as a double-decaf latté on a cold, rainy day.

"I know, Martha. I know. Thanks for understanding." Kenzie wiped her nose on her sleeve for the second time that day. "You're the best. I miss you."

"I miss you, too, hon," Martha said, with a catch in her voice. "We all do. If you get a notion to transfer back to UT, we'd all come out there and help you pack. But I've got a feeling you're going to do great at PCU. Just give it time. And be who you are. That's all God wants you to be."

"Thanks, Martha. Uh-oh, that's my other line beeping in—"

"You go, then…and call your dad! He's in his car—he forgot he had an appointment. Love you!"

"Love you, too."

Kenzie held the cordless phone away from her face and pushed a button to connect with the other call.

"Hello?"

"Is this the future PCU student body president and homecoming queen?" A deep Tennessee drawl boomed through the receiver, crackling with the sound of a cellular phone.

"Hi, Dad."

"Kenzie? How's my sweet baby girl?"

"Fine. Are you coming to Seattle, Dad?"

"Thought I would, since Billy's coming. It's gonna be a big show—Seattle's a big market for him, you know."

Kenzie knew full well. There was a lot about the Christian music business that Kenzie knew. *And wouldn't Emily just love to know it…or Chris.*

"I remember, Dad. The Mariners game. Billy brought me that cap, remember, after he sang the national anthem in the playoffs. I wear it all the time." *I don't tell people who gave it to me, but I wear it.*

"Well, I don't fly out to his shows much anymore, but I thought it would be a good excuse to take you out for a fabulous meal. Whattya say? Maybe we'll steal Billy away from his fans after the show. Or maybe I'll just hog my favorite daughter all to myself."

Kenzie smiled, knowing that her dad called each one of his four daughters "my favorite." It was a family joke, and one of the most endearing ones in his repertoire.

"That'd be great, Dad. I can't wait to see you."

"Call Martha to set aside some comps for your friends, honey. I'm sure there are some kids you'd like to bring, huh?"

Kenzie felt a tightening in the pit of her stomach. 'Comps' —free concert tickets with accompanying backstage passes— were one of the perks that often came along with the Kenzie Dawson Friendship Package.

"Uh, well, Dad, I think kids are already buying tickets. Is it okay if I just stay backstage with you, so we can get to dinner faster? It's not like I haven't seen the show already."

Okay, now I'm stretching the truth with my own father. I am absolutely incorrigible.

"Don't want to be seen hanging around with the old man,

huh?" Kenzie's dad was laughing as he said it, to her relief. "That's all right. I understand. Actually, that'll work out fine. Less trouble for the road manager. Maybe I can meet your friends later. But if you need tickets for anyone, tell Martha."

"Dad, Martha's not your assistant anymore, she's V.P. of administration. You keep forgetting."

"Well, she'd still do that for you, you know that, Keeks."

"I know," said Kenzie. "If my friends don't get tickets for some reason, I'll call her. Besides, Dad, most of the kids at PCU don't give a rip about Billy. He's not exactly the Seattle sound, you know. I mean, they've heard of him, but it's not like he's all over MTV or anything."

"And we're selling out arenas with this dorky VH-1 guy, whose new album just *debuted* at number fifteen on the *Billboard* sales chart, my dear child, even without MTV." Johnny Dawson's expansive manner contracted just a little in defense of Billy Weber, the artist he'd discovered, nurtured, and made into a bonafide crossover pop star.

"And I don't have to remind you that those platinum-album sales are helping to pay your way through college, now do I, my dear?"

"I know, Dad. I didn't mean anything by it. I just didn't want you to expect that all of my friends would be coming to the show." Kenzie paced back and forth in her eight-by-twelve foot room. She'd said the wrong thing. *Again.*

"Honey, I know that! Besides, I think we're about to sign a band that the college crowd is really gonna go for. Did you listen to that demo tape I sent you? I want you to give me your opinion. They're from the Seattle area, too, which is another reason why I'm coming.

"Dad? I gotta go…my roommates probably need to use the phone, and I've been on it for a while. Are you flying in the day of the show? I can come pick you up. Then we can just hang out at the arena or go eat or something. Is that okay?"

"Sounds good to me, Keeks. I'm going to try to talk your mother into coming, but she's awfully busy these days…what with her executive mentoring group and church and tennis and the Young Life board and the grandbabies. Little Parker is crawling now, you know."

"Well, kiss them all for me and tell everybody I miss 'em. Okay, Dad? Can't wait to see you. Love you, Pops."

"Love you, too, kiddo. Be good."

"I will! Bye."

Kenzie stopped pacing the room and slammed the antenna into the cordless phone with the palm of her hand. *Be good, he says. If he only knew.*

Opening the door to the hallway, Kenzie found Beth and Emily sitting cross-legged on the ugly avocado green couch, listening to Billy Weber's new CD and reading the lyrics from the CD insert.

"Beth's gonna go to the Billy Weber concert!" squealed Emily. "Isn't that great? You've gotta go, Kenzie! It's supposed to be his best tour *ever!*"

Kenzie had no doubt that Emily knew every detail about this tour—including the facts that Madonna's lighting company, Sting's sound engineer and Michael Jackson's former drummer had all been hired. Emily kept up on the latest in Christian music by reading fan magazines like *CCM* and *SHOUT,* and especially *RELEASE,* which was her favorite. She even clipped out articles and taped them to the back of her bedroom door, which Kenzie found slightly nauseating.

"Well, Em…looks like that's the very weekend my dad's coming in, so I guess you'll just have to go without me. Thanks for thinking of me, though. It sounds great!"

Afterward, Kenzie changed into baggy gym shorts and basketball Nikes and headed out for the gym, wincing at the half-truths she had just told.

So much for honesty, she thought, her stomach churning. *I must have lost those good intentions somewhere on the trail.*

8

Kenzie groaned. It wasn't supposed to be like this. Ever since she'd first thought of attending PCU, she'd looked forward to leaving behind the trappings and expectations that went along with being Johnny Dawson's youngest daughter.

How could she have forgotten that Billy Weber's ever-thriving career would bring him to Seattle, and that she'd be expected to attend his concert? Even worse was the knowledge that she could help Chris Gallagher—who she was liking more and more all the time—if she were to tell her influential father about him.

Such were the dilemmas facing Mary Mackenzie Dawson as she moved through her routine of going to classes, studying, and hanging out with friends, during the stretch of time between her dad's phone call and the day of the concert.

"Kenzie, when's your birthday? Isn't it Presidents' Day or something like that?"

Kenzie glanced over at Allie, who had dropped by on her way to the library and was flipping through the pages of the Winnie the Pooh calendar Emily had contributed to the suite's bare walls.

"Valentine's. February 14, in case you don't have the date written down." She was stretched out on the avocado couch, a U.S. history textbook open in her lap and a yellow highlighter pen in her hand.

"How weird is it having your birthday on Valentine's Day?" Allie wondered. "It's coming up, by the way." She plopped down in a chair, apparently giving up on the idea of going to the library.

"It is kinda strange. Mom always made it special, though. Always managed to pull off a good birthday for me without leaving out the romantic aspect for Dad."

"Well, speaking of romantic aspects..."

"Yes?" Kenzie stuck the cap of her highlighter pen in her mouth.

"You may be flirting with Chris, finally, but you aren't actually dating him yet, so we can't count on that for Valentine's Day. And your birthday can't be another G.N.O. like Emily's early birthday party was."

"Our Girls Night Out wasn't bad. Poor Em, though. Having a birthday on Christmas Eve is worse than Valentine's Day. At least I get to celebrate with my friends. Unless they're on hot dates."

"Well, no hot dates for me this year. I think we should have a Loser's Party for all of us who don't have Significant Others. We'll have to work on that. Or maybe *you* should just work on getting a Significant Other."

"If you're talking about Chris, I don't know what else you expect me to do. I've spent umpteen late nights at The Cup, pretending to study. Between that and Young Life on Fridays, we've been talking a lot."

"Well, maybe there's hope for you after all. As for me, I'm scoping on somebody who works at the library. See ya."

Allie picked up her backpack and headed for the door, snatching a can of root beer from the mini-fridge on the way out.

"That'll be seventy-five cents, Raju."

"Put it on my tab."

As it turned out, Kenzie didn't have much time to worry about her birthday and Valentine's Day. Between studying for classes, writing research papers, and trying to keep up with the reading for her Young Life Leadership meetings, Kenzie was one busy coed.

And there was the matter of Chris. The evenings Kenzie spent at The Cup were coming to fruition. When he saw Kenzie around campus, Chris almost always stopped to chat—an event that made Kenzie late for class on more than one occasion.

"Ken-zie!" Chris shouted across the quad one morning, as Kenzie was on her way to Dr. Sullivan's history class. She stopped as Chris jogged toward her. "Hey! I wanted to catch you before you went to class. Do you think—Um, you're not going to believe it, but they're showing *Little Women* at the Union tomorrow night, and I—" Chris was breathless from the short run.

"I know! I saw it in the paper!" Kenzie wanted to kick herself for interrupting him. *Let him ask you.*

"Well, I don't have to play at The Cup, and I was wondering—Uh, would you like to go?" He scraped the side of his hiking boot on the sidewalk, like a junior high schooler. Kenzie thought it was adorable.

"Sure! You won't be embarrassed about going to a chick flick?"

"As long as I don't see Ryan and those guys." Chris laughed

and pulled on the dangling straps of his backpack.

"I won't tell if you won't." Kenzie realized once again that she was flirting with a musician. *It's okay. This one's different.*

"Well, good. I'll call you. Gotta go now. I've been late to Biology three times in a row."

"Go! I'll talk to you later. Have a great day!" Kenzie watched him jog down the path, and wondered how in the world such a fine thing could be true. She was going to see *Little Women* with a guy she really liked!

On Thursday, it became a reality. *Little Women* made her cry, as it always did, and she was relieved to find that she wasn't embarrassed in front of Chris. Sitting next to him in the darkened auditorium, she sniffled and sopped up tears with a red bandanna, offered by Chris with a reassuring "It's clean, I just washed it."

When it was over, Kenzie and Chris joined the mostly female throng of moviegoers heading out the back door. In the light of the auditorium lobby, Kenzie squinted and blinked. Across the room, she spied Emily and her friend Dan, who knew Chris from a class.

"Hey, Em, Dan," Chris greeted them. "What's up?"

"Nothing." Dan nodded. "Hi, Kenzie. Did you like the movie, Chris?"

"Oh, yeah. I loved it. Made me cry all over again. Didn't you, Dan?"

"Especially when Beth dies?" Chris put on a sappy girl act, and Dan jumped right in with the mockery.

"Oh, Chris! What about when Professor Behr almost gets on the train without seeing Jo, because he thinks she's married to Laurie?"

"Oh, that was heart-wrenching. I didn't bring enough Kleenex, did you?"

"Stop." Emily socked Chris playfully on the arm, laughing. "Kenzie, where'd you get this guy?"

"Picked him up in a bar. Coffee bar, that is. Can't take him out in public though."

Wow! thought Kenzie. *Imagine that. I'm having fun, with Chris and Emily both! Things are definitely looking up.*

Kenzie's relationship with Chris continued to grow slowly and naturally, and she was glad. But there was still the matter of the Billy Weber concert, and Kenzie was determined to get through it with her integrity intact.

On Saturday, February 8, just after lunch, Kenzie found herself in Emily's room, trying to act interested as her suite-mate rifled through her closet trying to decide what to wear to the Big Concert.

"Should I wear my Billy Weber T-shirt with jeans? No, too cold. What about a skirt and a turtleneck and my Billy Weber denim tour jacket?"

Try "too dorky," thought Kenzie, stifling the urge to scream.

"I can't believe it! This concert is going to be *so great!* Did you hear he's got this conveyor belt he runs on, in the middle of the arena? I can't *wait* to see it!" Emily gushed. Kenzie thought she saw an actual shudder of delight run through her roommate's body. *How can she be so normal, until she starts talking about Billy Weber or Christian music in general?*

The loud, electronic purr of Kenzie's phone gave her an excuse to dash out of the room.

"Dawson's Dunk-'em Donuts, may ah hep you?" Kenzie answered in a sitcom-style, exaggerated Southern accent.

"Kenzie? Is that you, honey? I'll take a dozen, then." The well-loved voice at the other end was masked by static interference.

"Oh, hi, Dad! Where are you?"

"About thirty thousand feet above Colorado. Let's see, I think that's Boulder down there…"

"Oh, *Dad!*" Kenzie groaned, in feigned exasperation. She could just imagine her father in his first-class aisle seat, leaning over the guy in the window seat to take a look, just to be funny.

"Listen, kiddo, I'm not going to be able to meet you at school, if that's okay with you. Somebody from the *Seattle Times* wants to interview me, if you can believe it, along with Billy. For the business section, I think. Can you meet me at the arena after sound check?"

At that moment, Emily bounced into Kenzie's room, modeling the jeans-turtleneck-denim jacket combo she'd picked out for the evening's concert wear. *It just screams Billy Weber Psycho-Fan,* Kenzie thought, trying not to roll her eyes.

"Uh, yeah, Dad—that's great, actually." Kenzie was now aware that her conversation could be heard by her excitable roommate. "What time?"

"How about four-thirty? We had to stay in Nashville an extra day for an award thing, so Billy will be there just in time for sound check. He's right here; hold on, he wants to talk to you."

Kenzie smiled wryly. *If Emily knew who this was, her screams could be heard all the way to the Canadian border.*

"Hey, Kenzie. How are you, girl? Those college guys treating you right? If they're not, you tell me about it, and I'll work 'em over." Hearing Billy's familiar, friendly voice, Kenzie felt a stab of remorse for hiding the truth about their long-time friendship.

"That's scary. What're you doin', you goofball? How're Susan and the kids?" Kenzie smiled, then grimaced. Billy's biggest fan was within earshot, and she had just dropped a huge hint as to who was on the other end of the phone. *You are so paranoid,* Kenzie told herself. *As if Em even has a CLUE…*

"They're great. Told me to give you their love. Hey, can't wait to see you! Are you bringing your friends to the show?"

"They'll be there…" Once again, Kenzie heard herself telling a half-truth.

"Great! Bring your friends backstage after the show, if you want to. Hey, listen, here's your dad—see you later!" Billy sounded rested and pumped up for a big evening. Kenzie surmised—not wanting to ask and tip off Emily—that he must have had a couple of days in Nashville, off the tour.

"Keeks, you're gonna love the show; it's really happenin'." Kenzie wondered if other people's dads used the word "happenin'" in normal conversation.

"Well, cool. Um, Dad, isn't this phone like six bucks a minute? Tell me where to meet you."

"All righty. Listen, did you get that laminate Martha Fed-Exed you?"

"Yeah, Dad, I did." Getting a FedEx package at her dorm room had been a tough one to explain to the ever-curious Emily. Tougher still was finding a private moment in which she could open the package which contained her plastic, laminated "all-access" badge. *If Emily knew I had this…*

"You remember the drill. Show your laminate at backstage parking, then get somebody from the crew to find me or Billy. Did I say four-thirty? Come backstage, to Billy's dressing room. Bye, honey, I love you."

"Love you, too. Bye, Dad."

Kenzie clicked the off button on the cordless phone and set it on the bed, where Emily had seated herself.

"Who were you talking to? Besides your dad, I mean? Was he really calling you from the airplane? Wow!" Emily was all ears.

"Yeah, he was. It's kinda cool 'til you get the phone bill." Kenzie wanted it to sound like her dad actually looked at—and cared about—his phone bills.

Deflecting Emily's other question, Kenzie swallowed hard and offered an opinion on the outfit without Emily having to ask. "You look totally cute, but—" She thought for a moment, trying to figure out how to get Emily to leave the Billy Weber paraphernalia at home. "Do you think you'll be warm enough with just a jean jacket?"

"Well, I'd rather be cold than miss a chance to wear this jacket to the concert! Ryan bought it for me—as an early birthday present—when Billy came to Portland on his last tour. That was the best! My best friend Holly and I got his autograph. I had him sign my sleeve! See?" Emily held up her jacketed arm for Kenzie's perusal. "He was *soooo* nice! We took our picture with him, too."

"Well, isn't that something!" Kenzie hoped she sounded adequately impressed.

"Too bad you can't go with us, Kenzie. It's going to be a great show. I know you'd like it!"

"Yeah, well…I'm sure I would. Y'all have a great time, and maybe Dad and I will catch you after dinner. At The Cup, maybe."

In a fit of Billy Weber-inspired enthusiasm, Emily gave Kenzie a quick half-hug and practically skipped out of the room.

Kenzie breathed a quick prayer. *Oh, Lord, help me. Help me not to kill her before she finishes her freshman year. And help her not to kill me when she finds out what I've been keeping from her…*

9

By four o'clock, Kenzie had changed into nice jeans, boots, and the cashmere sweater she'd worn to The Cup on her first night back from Christmas break, one month earlier. Kenzie pulled her Jeep out of the lot and wound her way out of the confines of PCU, down the hilly U-District streets, toward the Key Arena, on the site of the 1962 World's Fair. She'd been there before, and with her fine sense of direction, she found the arena's parking area in no time.

Soon, she spotted the familiar tour buses and huge tractor-trailer rigs, backed up to the stage loading area. The road crew guys—wearing ponytails, black leather tennis shoes, and T-shirts bearing the names of obscure rock bands—were busily hefting to the stage huge boxes filled with T-shirts, jean jackets, and tour books.

Kenzie knew what it took to make a concert like Billy's come together. She was aware that crews of riggers had been up early, setting up the stage for the sound and light crews to come in after and do their magic: hard, physical work that would help create the astounding atmosphere that made a Billy Weber concert a real event. In the late afternoon, the opening acts and

Billy's band—including Billy—had shown up to run through bits of songs, allowing the sound engineers to set up proper levels at the sound board, tweak microphone placements, and double and triple-check all the equipment.

Kenzie set out on her quest to find the road manager, Jack Colton, who would know exactly where she could find her dad and Billy. It was Jack's job to know those things, and he did it better than anyone in the business.

But first, Kenzie had to get through the local security guys. Sure enough, a beefy six-footer made his way toward her as she tried to park her Jeep in a VIP space.

"I'm sorry, you can't park there without a pass."

Kenzie stuck her laminated badge through the open window. "My dad's the president of Billy Weber's record company—Johnny Dawson. I'm meeting him backstage at 4:30."

The burly, black-shirted guard looked at the badge and frowned. "You're gonna hafta talk to the road manager. He's got the list."

Kenzie spotted Jack Colton striding across the loading ramp with a clipboard in one hand and a walkie-talkie in the other. "Wait, there he is! Colton! Over here!" She waved frantically till she got his attention, which was tough, considering all the commotion that was going on around him.

"Kenzie! You little…"

Jack Colton hopped off the loading ramp as Kenzie jumped out of the Jeep. As he met her, he swept Kenzie off her feet in a brotherly hug.

"Looking for your daddy? He's looking for you! So's Billy. Come on. I'll take you to the dressing room. Sound check's running on time, believe it or not."

Kenzie believed it. Jack Colton ran the road show like a well-oiled machine.

As they walked past the beefy security guard who'd stopped

her in the parking lot, Kenzie flashed him a grin and a "thumbs-up" sign, which he sheepishly returned. She never faulted the security guards for doubting her reasons for being there; she was a teenage girl, and thus a prime candidate for "crazed-fan" status. *They're trying to save Billy from people like Emily,* she thought, then felt guilty for thinking it.

As they walked down the long, grimy yellow cement-block corridor, Kenzie got a whiff of something that smelled delicious. Peeking into one side room, she spotted her favorite backstage perk: the pre-show, catered buffet, provided so the musicians and crew could eat at their convenience. Like most major artists, Billy's road show included a fairly impressive dinner at every performance. Some were better than others. This one looked and smelled like a winner.

"Is that baked salmon?" Kenzie asked Jack. "I can't believe it. The promoter went all out, huh?"

"It's salmon, all right. Fresh out of the Pacific, no doubt. Jerry Garfield goes all out for Billy when he promotes the Seattle shows, since it's Jerry's hometown. Hires a great chef. Kind of spoils us."

Kenzie made a mental note to come back for a taste later on.

Walking fast down the cavernous, tunnel-like hallway, Kenzie heard her dad's laughter and felt her heart skip a beat. Despite her confusion about leaving Nashville and "finding her own way," Kenzie loved her dad like no one else. Hearing his voice made her realize how much she missed him, workaholic tendencies and all.

"Keeks!" Dad had spotted her. Kenzie walked fast toward the booming voice. She wanted to run, but it just wasn't cool.

Before she knew it, Kenzie was engulfed in a bear-like hug. The familiar scent of her dad's after-shave gave her a sense of comfort and belonging that she hadn't felt in Seattle since her folks had left the SEA-TAC airport at the beginning of the semester.

How could I possibly not be proud to be his daughter? Suddenly, Kenzie felt the urge to cry on her daddy's shoulder. She stifled the urge and pulled away from his hug to look at him. "Dad, I've missed you," she said, her eyes stinging from the pent-up tears.

"Well, honey, it's only been a month since you've been home. Do you want to move back? University of Tennessee's got a good forestry program, I hear." Johnny Dawson's cobalt-blue eyes twinkled with the joke. Seeing his wide, toothpaste-commercial smile and his silvery white hair curling around his collar, Kenzie felt a twinge of tenderness that momentarily melted away all her confusion.

"That's okay, Dad. I'm fine. Really! PCU is great." Kenzie tried hard to look like she meant it, even though the thought of the Knoxville campus and weekends at their Smoky Mountains cabin sounded very appealing all of a sudden.

"Well, I'm looking forward to seeing your friends."

"So am I, girl!" Suddenly, Billy Weber popped out from around the door of his dressing room, and swept Kenzie up in yet another bear hug.

"Gosh, it's good to see you! So did you bring your friends to the show? It's great—the band is really hot this tour."

Kenzie kissed Billy on the cheek and looked at him, handsome as a movie star, even in his pre-shower, "road-dog" grubbiness.

"Actually, they're coming on their own. They'd already bought tickets."

"Well, bring 'em backstage to the meet-and-greet if you want to," he offered, referring to the pre-concert promotional event that was staged for special guests, concert promoters, and radio station personnel.

"Or bring them back after the show," interjected Jack Colton, who looked like he needed to be somewhere else. "We're doing a little autograph thing tonight—for the big Christian radio station. Seattle's got one of the best, you know."

Kenzie knew. Emily listened to it constantly, when she wasn't playing Christian CDs. "Maybe…"

It's going to happen, Kenzie thought. Emily will find Billy, I know it. The cat will be out of the bag. She'll go ballistic. My life will be miserable and I really will *have to transfer to UT. But at least it won't be a secret anymore. Oh, no—what about Chris? He'd want to meet Billy for sure, but he's too shy—good grief!*

Kenzie smiled and thanked Jack for the info, as he took off in a quick stride down the corridor, barking instructions into his walkie-talkie. "See ya later!" he yelled to Kenzie, from halfway down the hall.

Suddenly, it occurred to her that Billy just might do something terribly embarrassing on stage—like say something to an "old friend who lives in Seattle." It would be just like him to be that folksy and casual, especially during the acoustic set, where the band went off stage and Billy sat on a stool with his guitar, under one spotlight. It was the most personal part of the concert, and there was no telling what he might be inclined to say. It was entirely possible that Billy could innocently, unintentionally blow Kenzie's "cover."

"Hey, Billy?"

"Yes?"

"Um, you're probably not going to do this. I mean, you probably didn't think about it at all, but…um…don't take this wrong or anything, but when you do the acoustic set, could you not mention…I mean—"

Billy interrupted her verbal fumbling with a laugh. "Do you mean, 'Billy, don't say anything embarrassing about me'? Like,

'Hey, I've got a special friend here in Seattle that I'd like to dedicate this song to, that cute girl with the brown hair and dimples in the fourth row, and I used to change her diapers, and her name's Kenzie Dawson.' That sort of thing?"

Kenzie relaxed instantly. "Ahh…yeah," she chuckled. "That sort of thing. I'd appreciate it."

"Don't worry. I'll be a good boy. I promise. Besides, Susan already made me say I wouldn't embarrass you. By the way, she sent some cookies for you. Too bad, though. We ate them on the plane."

Kenzie punched Billy's arm, hard, like she'd been doing ever since her dad had first signed him to a record deal. "Billy Weber, you did not! You better hand those cookies over right now, or I'm going to give your hotel phone number to all the psycho fans in Seattle!" She cringed, thinking that the most psycho one of all lived in her suite at the dorm.

"I'm kidding, Kenz. Your dad has them, I think. If *he* hasn't eaten them. Hey, speaking of eating…how about going for Thai food after the show? Right now, I've got to go finish up sound check. See you later, kid?"

Billy held up his palm for a "high-five," which Kenzie slapped just before he jogged down the hall toward the stage.

The three hours before showtime went by fast, and Kenzie bumped into at least a dozen acquaintances from Nashville. At the pre-concert "meet-and-greet," much to Kenzie's relief, there was no sign of Emily, or anyone else from PCU. *Thank goodness. I'm spared another moment.*

The concert went off without a hitch. The opening bands were a big hit, and later on Key Arena rocked with the sounds of thousands of fans swaying, clapping, stomping and singing along to Billy's hits, accompanied by his best band yet. The state-of-the-art sound and lighting systems, along with high-tech special effects and video razzle-dazzle, gave the crowd exactly what they'd been looking for: a full-on pop concert as good as any show anywhere, but with the conviction and purpose of Billy's encouraging, Christian-themed music and lyrics.

But it was during the acoustic set that Billy had the audience eating out of his hand. Much to Kenzie's relief, he honored her half-joking "please don't embarrass me" request. Feeling more relaxed, Kenzie ventured out from behind backstage, coming to one of the side arena entrances for an audience-eye view at the show. With that many Billy Weber fans in the Key Arena, the chances of seeing Emily and the gang were slim, and Kenzie really did want to see the lights and special effects. Most of all, she wanted to hear what the audience was hearing, instead of the off-balance, backstage sound mix bouncing off the walls of the arena.

These basketball arenas aren't meant for music, thought Kenzie. *I wish Billy could scale down and play the concert halls again.*

After the show—which finished to three standing, stomping, and shouting ovations—Kenzie hung around backstage and waited for her dad. The thought of a great Thai meal, with Dad at the ordering helm, had her mouth watering. She was more relaxed and happy than she'd imagined she'd be. Her usually unruly stomach was actually calm and, as she thought to herself with a laugh, "fit to be Thaid."

While she was waiting, Kenzie noticed a group of high schoolers gathered at the front of the stage area, with a cadre of black-shirted security beefers hovering nearby. Jack Colton was there, too, with his attaché and radio. And next to him was Billy: drenched in sweat and radiant after a great performance. *This must be that autograph thing Jack was talking about.*

As she watched, Billy signed hats, posters, T-shirts and the colorful, glossy tour programs for twenty minutes. The security guards kept the small, apparently select crowd in a single-file line, awaiting their turn with Billy.

Kenzie was about to go off in search of a Coke and her father when she heard a familiar shriek. "Hi, Billy! I just wanted to tell you that I *love* your new CD! I think it's the best one you've ever done. I play it all the time! I have a radio show on campus at Pacific Cascades, KPCU…and I had a Billy-Thon to promote the show."

Yikes.

Kenzie could only stare. Emily, wearing the denim Billy Weber jacket, was out of control: wigged out, fritzed, over the edge, as far as Kenzie was concerned, though she wasn't really as bad as some other fans. Kenzie had seen it happen a thousand times. Kids who were normally sane could completely lose it when in the presence of an admired celebrity. Billy was used to enthusiastic reactions, though. He smiled kindly and thanked Emily for promoting him on her show. Emily beamed, held up the other sleeve for his signature and practically screamed the words Kenzie had imagined only in her worst nightmare:

"Billy, my suite-mate is from Nashville! Could I get an extra autograph for her? She's not here, she had to go someplace with her dad. Her name's Kenzie Dawson—"

Hearing that, Kenzie wished her dad was right next to her to hold her up, instead of fifty feet away, chatting with a band member. She plastered herself against the concrete wall near the side of the stage and waited breathlessly for Billy's response.

Billy looked at Emily in confusion. "What do you mean? Kenzie and her dad were here just before the show. Where'd they go?"

10

If Billy and her dad hadn't been so understanding, Kenzie wouldn't have been able to touch a bite of her Pad Thai or her chili-garlic shrimp. The Unfortunate Emily Incident, as she referred to it at dinner, was handled much better by Billy than it was by Kenzie. While Kenzie had remained in the shadows, too shocked to move, Billy had made a graceful recovery, explaining to a confused Emily that he was sure it was all a simple misunderstanding. To Kenzie's surprise, Billy wasn't a bit offended by her reticence to acknowledge their friendship to her friends at PCU.

"I'm sorry I spilled the beans for you, 'specially since I knew how you felt," he said, tipping his bowl away to collect the last spoonful of Tom Ka Kai, the delectable lemon grass-coconut-chicken soup they all loved. "We've all known since before you left. Did you think you had us fooled? You didn't come to PCU for the football team, that's for sure."

"Or the forestry department, either, Keeks," Johnny Dawson said, scooping a big helping of garlic beef onto a pile of sticky white rice. "If you wanted forestry, you could have gone to UT

120

and interned with the park rangers in the Smokies. You know that. We knew that, too. But we let you go, anyway. We knew you had to find your own way."

It was almost too much for Kenzie to bear. They understood.

"Your friend—what's her name? Emily?—was a nice girl, Kenzie," said Billy. "But I've got a feeling that when you go back to the dorm..." Billy broke into his best Ricky Ricardo imitation: "You've got some 'splainin' to do, Lucy..."

"Do I *ever*. I've been such a jerk." Kenzie put her fork down and cradled her face in her hands.

"Honey, it's okay," Kenzie's dad reached over and squeezed his youngest daughter's shoulder. "You've just been trying to be somebody you're not, that's all. Or...trying not to be somebody that you are, I guess, is more like it. I know it's not easy being my baby girl, especially in Nashville. People expect things out of you. Or maybe you don't think they like you for who you are? Maybe you're not sure if they are trying to be your friends because of who you know. Is that it?"

Kenzie stared down at the table for a minute, then looked up and pulled her hair back out of her face, blinking tears. There at the table were the two men she loved most in the world. They were being so understanding...*I just don't deserve this.*

"Did you think that Mom and I didn't know why you wanted to go so far away? We didn't want you to, of course—especially your mom, with you being the baby and all. But we knew you had to test your wings, if you know what I mean."

Yes, Dad. I know exactly what you mean. Kenzie couldn't bring herself to speak the words that were right on the tip of her tongue. She was afraid she would burst into sobs and make a scene.

"Johnny, I don't mean to interrupt, but—"

"It's okay, Billy. Go on." Johnny Dawson looked at Billy with a fatherly affection that transcended their professional relationship.

"Kenzie, I know it has to be hard for you, especially here, where people aren't use to having artists as neighbors and friends. Maybe this has had the opposite effect on you, huh? At least in Nashville, you'd see me at the grocery store and not hide behind the potato chip rack."

"Like you ever actually go to the grocery store." Even in a tender moment, Kenzie could manage a playful dig.

"Yeah, well…" Billy grinned sheepishly.

"I know what you're saying, Billy. I never thought about it before till just now, but you're right. At least in Nashville, I'm not the only one with famous friends. Or a semi-famous father."

"Gee, thanks, dear daughter," laughed Mr. Dawson. "You better watch it, kiddo, or I'm writing you out of the will."

Kenzie sighed in gratitude for the comic relief. Still, she couldn't believe that something this big to her seemed so inconsequential to her dad and Billy.

"You mean you're not mad?" She looked at them for signs of hidden anger or disappointment, but all she saw was love and acceptance.

"No, honey, we're not mad," said Mr. Dawson. "Neither is your mom, in case you were wondering…although she wouldn't mind having you back in Tennessee, that's for sure."

"You mean, this whole time, you knew why I wanted to get away? How come you never said anything before?" Uncharacteristically, Kenzie let her noodles sit, virtually untouched.

"Aren't you going to eat your Pad Thai?" Kenzie's dad didn't wait for an answer, but helped himself to a good portion from her plate. "Yes, honey, we knew. Of course we knew. But you had to figure this out yourself. So did your sisters, by the way, especially Anna Kristin. Billy was the hottest thing when she was in college, remember?"

"Yeah. I'm not 'alternative' enough for you kids now," laughed Billy. "Especially not you cool Seattle college types. Except maybe a few—like your roommate, I guess."

"Kenzie, sweetheart…" Mr. Dawson looked at his daughter with compassion in his eyes. "Whatever you want to do is okay with Mom and me, you know that…as long as it doesn't hurt you. And we thought that giving you the freedom to go all the way across country might help you. Besides, PCU is a good place. Even if it does have a lousy football team." He gave Kenzie one of his trademark smiles, and signaled for the waiter.

"Want your Pad Thai heated up, hon? You haven't eaten much. Do you want something else? How 'bout some barbe-cued squid?"

"No thanks, Dad, there's plenty here…" Feeling her appetite begin to come back, Kenzie took her fork and dug into the lukewarm plate of Thai noodles and spicy peanut sauce.

"Dad, I have to tell you something. My friends think you're a corporate executive or something. I've been really…vague."

"Well, I *am* a corporate executive or something! It's not such a big deal, Kenz. Would you be embarrassed if I were an insur-ance salesman, or a pastor, or a mailman? You could just say I was a studio musician. Used to be, anyway."

"Dad, I'd be proud of you, whatever you did…except, I haven't seemed very proud of you if I won't tell people what you do, about LightSong and everything." Kenzie wouldn't let her father's assurances close the subject. She wanted to be good and sure that he knew everything.

"Dad, there's more to it than that. You know that place I told you about, The Cup and Chaucer?"

"Yes. Should we go there for coffee and dessert tonight?" Mr. Dawson pulled out his billfold and placed a platinum credit card on the plastic tray. A waiter soon appeared to whisk it away. Within seconds, he was back, and Mr. Dawson signed the credit card slip. Kenzie knew he'd left a huge tip; the waiter was smiling and thanking him profusely.

"Well, no, Dad. Maybe next time. But, see, there's this guy that plays there. His name's Chris—"

"OH!" Billy perked up immediately. "NOW we're getting somewhere! Johnny, I think there's love in the air."

"*Billy.* There's more to it than that. Although there is *that.* You see, Dad, Billy…he's a…a…a musician."

Billy covered his mouth with his hands in mock alarm, while Mr. Dawson feigned a heart attack, pounding his chest with his fist. "No! Not one of *those!*" he teased. "Quick, Weber—to The Cup and Chaucer at once! We must rescue my daughter from the clutches of this evil creature. He must be stopped!"

The two men got up from the table and headed toward the door.

"*Da*-ad…" Kenzie grabbed his arm and gave him a "you are *so* weird" look: the kind only a teenager can deliver with the proper effect. "I'm serious. He's really good, Dad. I mean *scary* good. And he doesn't know it. And I haven't said anything to him, I mean, I haven't said much of anything to him at all, and…"

By the time Kenzie finished explaining "the Chris thing," they had gotten the Jeep out of the restaurant parking garage and were halfway to the hotel. With the lights of the city sparkling in the softly falling rain, Kenzie found herself gazing as she talked and drove, while Billy, exhausted from his nearly athletic concert performance, fell asleep in the back seat.

This really is a great city, she mused. *I have a lot to learn here.*

"So, Kenzie, when can I hear this kid? Does he have anything on tape? You know we're checking out a new band near here, anyway. If he's as good as you say, I'd like to give him a listen. You've got a great ear, kiddo. Just like your old man, I've always said."

Kenzie's dad was looking right at her, not the city lights. She could tell that he missed being able to ride in the Jeep with his "favorite daughter," the "best driver in the family."

"Well, yeah…" Kenzie hoped he couldn't see her blush in the dark. "I think he's probably got a little four-track in his room, maybe an old Tascam or something. He loves vintage equipment, by the way." Kenzie could speak recording lingo as well as anybody, having practically grown up in the studio, at her daddy's knee. Hearing the words come out of her own mouth made her realize that she missed hanging out while he or Billy was working on a recording project.

"Well, then…send me something. If you ever get the nerve to talk to him about it, that is."

"Okay, Dad. I will."

"Keeks…this Chris thing doesn't have anything to do with ol' bad boy Dylan Frost, does it? Remember, not all musicians are flakes. I mean, your mom did all right with one, don't you think?"

Kenzie couldn't believe her ears. The blush in her cheeks turned to hot crimson.

"Sure. Uh, Dad? Could we talk about this later? I mean, Billy needs to get to his room, obviously." Kenzie had stopped the Jeep in front of the hotel where Mr. Dawson and Billy were staying. Billy, under the relaxing influence of a sumptuous Thai meal, was just waking up from his mini-nap in the back seat.

"Honey…just remember that whatever you do is okay with your mom and me. If you want to date a musician, date a musician. And may I remind you, young lady, that you're no slouch of a musician yourself. Are you playing much out here?"

"Well, no, not really." Kenzie shrugged and slumped tiredly over the steering wheel as her dad got out of the Jeep and walked around to her window.

"Same reason as the rest of it, kiddo? I understand." Mr. Dawson shook his head gently, and his hair shone in the hotel lights like spun silver. "But you've got natural talent, and you know what the Lord had to say about that…so don't hide it, honey. Besides, I know you love it. Maybe you and this Chris kid could make a little duet thing happen, hmmm?"

"Dad!"

"Well, get out here and give your ol' Dad a big ol' hug and kiss…I guess I won't be seeing you tomorrow; I've got to catch an early flight, so I'll get a cab."

Kenzie hugged Billy first, then she hung onto her dad for dear life, relishing the comfort of knowing that she hadn't hurt his feelings with the deception she'd lived with all year at school.

"I love you, kiddo." Mr. Dawson gave his daughter a quick kiss and a pinch to her dimpled cheek. "Be good. And send me some of that kid's tunes. After you start talking to him, that is. If he's like all the guys in Nashville, he's already got it bad for you."

"Yeah right, Dad." Kenzie rolled her eyes, mostly because her dad expected it. "Thanks for dinner; it was great…and I love you too, Dad. See ya, Billy—awesome show! Really! And thanks for the talk, both of you. Guess I better go face the music with Emily, so to speak. Bye, love you!"

Kenzie hopped in the Jeep and pulled away, leaving her father and a very tired Billy Weber waving good-bye from under the covered valet entrance of the hotel.

"Wow," Kenzie said aloud. "That went way better than I thought it would. Why did I think it was going to be so bad? Maybe it won't be so bad with Emily, either."

Lighthearted and full of Pad Thai and warm feelings, Kenzie whistled her way back to campus in the Jeep. She whistled as she walked across campus from the parking lot to her dorm, and she whistled all the way up the stairs to the door of her suite.

It was a Billy Weber song…about honesty.

11

It was late when Kenzie got back to her suite, but all the lights were on, and there was music playing in the living room. Billy Weber music, of course. This time, though, she didn't mind it. This time, she was at peace with her conscience, untortured by thoughts of suite-mates who could pester the daylights out of her for knowing Billy Weber. Now it was different. Kenzie had come clean with Billy and her dad. Emily was another matter. Kenzie decided to think positively and take the upbeat approach.

She walked confidently into the living room and plopped down on the avocado couch, greeting her suite-mates with the friendliest tone she'd used all year.

"Hey, y'all! How'd you like the concert?"

The emotional temperature in the room dropped fifty degrees in three seconds. Emily turned around from her post at the window and gave an icy stare that made Kenzie shiver. *Dang it. Wrong approach, obviously.*

"So that's why you were so rude to me all semester. That's why you wouldn't tell me what you got in the mail. That's why you left the room when I had Billy's CD on. Kenzie, I thought you were my friend, but I was obviously wrong. A friend doesn't lie like that." Emily got choked up and walked into her room.

Kenzie froze. Beth looked at her and shrugged. "Whatever," she said, walking out of the suite. "I'm going to Brad's. Later."

Out of the blue, Kenzie remembered the verse from Proverbs that she'd underlined in her Bible the night before: "The Lord despises lying lips, but loves the truth."

Taking a deep breath, Kenzie got up off couch and eased into Emily's room, tapping softly on the door as she entered. She sat gingerly on the edge of Emily's bed where Emily was hunched up by her pillows, hugging her knees. Kenzie felt the urge to pace around the room, or worse, leave and go for a long run. *Lord, give me the courage to tell the truth.*

"Em, I'm sorry." She waited for a response, but none came. "Okay, so, here's the deal…I've been, um—" *Say it, girl.* "I've been lying to you. All semester. All year. Ever since I met you. I mean, not lying on purpose, just not telling you the truth. I just didn't…well, I didn't think it would be good if you knew that I knew Billy Weber. I didn't know how you would feel—"

Emily looked up at her suite-mate, appalled.

"I feel like a fool, that's how I feel, if you want to know!" she spouted. Kenzie had never seen this side of her normally sweet-tempered suite-mate. "Okay, so I'm a big Billy Weber fan. So what? Why couldn't you have shared him with your friends? Did you think we weren't good enough?"

Kenzie sat, dumfounded.

"You didn't think it would be *good*? I'm so *sure!* What did you think I would do, follow you home to Tennessee? Or bug you till you gave me Billy's home phone number? Do you really think I'm that much of a dweeb, Kenzie?" Emily's eyes were like neon lights, flashing hurt and anger.

"No!" Kenzie protested. "That's not it. You're really a great person. And lately I've been realizing how much we have in common. It's just that your excitement about Christian music—especially Billy's—makes me uncomfortable, that's all." Kenzie pulled nervously on her hair and looked at the Billy Weber poster on the wall.

"I guess I need to come clean with you. I know you think I'm a jerk, and you have a right to. I don't know if I can explain this in a way you'd understand—"

"You don't think I'd understand? Why, because I'm not as cool as you?" In a moment, Emily's anger shook loose into sobs.

Kenzie breathed a desperate prayer for divine intervention. *Oh, God, help me…what do I do? What do I say?*

"I'm sorry, Em. It's been really hard for me, too. I know you can't imagine that, but it *has* been. It's not as cool as you think, being so close to the Christian music scene. People like Billy are just people, you know. They just happen to be talented. And famous. But they can be jerks, too, you know. Like me, I guess."

Emily kept crying, but perked up a little at Kenzie's confession.

"Em, let me tell you something. Maybe it'll help you understand me better. Do you see that poster on your wall?"

Kenzie pointed at the poster of Billy, who looked sincere and wholesomely sexy.

"Do you know how much they discussed which photos to choose for the poster? Like whether he should be smiling or not? Did you know that the record company—yes, the one my family owns—goes to great lengths to make an artist's image appealing, so that someone like you will be convinced to buy his latest CD? Is there anything wrong with that? Maybe, maybe not. But you bought it, and you think Billy is cute, don't you?"

"What does that have to do with anything?" Emily asked, through her tears.

Kenzie got up and paced around the room, like a defense lawyer in front of a jury. "You buy Billy's album, because you like the music, which you've heard on your Christian radio station, and also because you love Billy's other CDs, right? Well, so here's this pretty talented guy, who also happens to be cute, and charming, and *married*, with three kids, and you put his pictures on the wall.

"And it just so happens that I know him, and have known him for a long time, and this whole celebrity image thing gets very caught up in my life because of that—which is why I cringed when I found out you were a big Billy Weber fan. I thought that maybe you would want to be my friend just because I knew him and because—well, maybe that would make you feel uncomfortable around me, and like you should be cooler than you are. Not that you aren't cool! I mean, Em, *I'm just me!* It doesn't matter who I know or who my parents are!"

Emily looked up, dry-eyed and stunned, to find Kenzie staring at her, ready to cry.

"Is *that* what this is all about, Kenzie? Why didn't you say so a long time ago?"

Just then, the sound of Cooper's laughter came from the hall as she and Ryan made a rambunctious entrance into the suite.

"Man on the floor! Hey, Em! Heard you got to talk to your buddy Billy Weber! So, how was—"

Cooper stopped her boisterous greeting when she detected the high emotion in the room.

"Uh-oh. Did we interrupt something? I'm sorry—"

"Well, yes, you did," said Kenzie. "But that's okay—maybe

it's even good. Coop, Ryan, I have a confession to make, and I might as well just spit it all out at the same time. You better sit down."

Cooper and Ryan exchanged perplexed looks and found seats on the edge of Cooper's bed.

"First of all, I'm not kidding about any of this. I'm totally serious. Here's the deal: My dad's not just a 'corporate executive.' He and my mom started a big Christian record company, LightSong Records, which my family still owns. It's the one Billy Weber's with. In fact, my dad discovered Billy Weber. He's been a good friend of our family since I was a kid. And I feel awful, because I've never told you that before."

Cooper looked long and hard at Kenzie, then at Emily, who still appeared stunned by Kenzie's confession.

"Okay. So?" Cooper sounded confused. "And?"

"Well, I feel terrible."

"Why? Because your family owns a Christian record company? What's wrong with that?"

"Nothing's wrong with it. But I've hurt Em's feelings. And I've lied to y'all, and to myself, really. As much as I've prayed about it, I still haven't been honest about it. Until tonight, that is."

Cooper was still baffled. "What is there to be honest about?"

"Well, for starters, I said I wasn't going to the concert, but I did—I was backstage the whole time, with my dad. And I could have invited y'all back there, too—actually, y'all could've had free tickets."

"*Free tickets?*" Ryan jumped into the fray. "Okay, so now *I'm* bummed." His grin subsided quickly when he noticed that neither his sister nor Kenzie looked amused. "Whoa. This is a girl thing, isn't it? Do I need to go?"

"No, it's not a girl thing. It's just a *me* thing." Kenzie gazed thoughtfully at Ryan, and wondered what it might have been like to have such an understanding brother—or to have a brother at all. "Ry, remember in the truck that night when you asked me about Billy's concert? I didn't tell you the truth. Well, I didn't exactly lie, but I may as well have. And when you told me about the cookies, well—"

Kenzie interrupted herself and glanced in Emily's direction. It was Ryan, not Emily, who had mentioned the cookies Emily sent to Billy. *Uh-oh. Embarrassing Emily could only make matters worse.* But Emily didn't flinch.

"Yes, I did send cookies to his record company—*your* record company, I mean. So what happened? Did somebody there eat them? Or did they get thrown away? You can tell me. I can take it." Emily was exhibiting a new strength in the midst of this "True Confessions" session, and it both heartened and surprised Kenzie.

"*Cookies,* Em?" Kenzie stared at her suite-mate.

Emily grinned and rolled her eyes. "Are you thinking that maybe I should get a life?"

"Or at least a down payment on one." Kenzie laughed and signaled Emily for a high-five. For the first time ever, the two connected in a gesture they'd both done a million times with other friends. It was a moment.

"Kenzie, you know what? I was just as embarrassed about sending those cookies as you are thinking about it," Emily admitted. "Really. Now that I've met Billy—twice—I kind of cringe thinking about how stupid that was. Like he would actually get cookies and actually eat them, from a fan. Remember, I was still in high school at the time."

"Like you're so mature now, right?" Ryan said, mockingly. "Big college freshman?"

Finally, Kenzie thought. *Ryan: The Perfect Brother is actually showing signs of being a pain.*

Kenzie walked over to where Ryan was leaning against the wall. With the fierce expression of a female warrior defending her tribal sister, she reared back and delivered a solid right cross to Ryan's left arm, causing him to yelp like a wounded animal. *"Ouch!* Hey! What're you doing? That hurt!"

"Serves you right, Buster! Don't be talkin' to my suite-mate that way, or I'll give you another one!" Kenzie held up her clenched fists and danced around like a prizefighter, ready to throw a punch. "C'mon, you wimp. I'll take ya ten rounds."

Emily jumped up, howling with delight at Kenzie's unexpected sisterly horseplay. "Tickle him! He's ticklish under his arms!"

That did it. All the tension of the last few hours dissipated into a frenzied attack on Emily's brother. "Dog-pile on Ryan!" Kenzie, Emily and Cooper wrestled him onto Emily's bed where Cooper and Kenzie held down his arms, giving Emily the pleasure of torturing her brother with merciless tickling.

"Okay, I give!" Ryan begged for release from his feminine captors. "I give! I'm sorry I said it…whatever I said! Stop! Stop! I was just kidding!"

Weak from the struggle to keep the athletic Ryan pinned down, the girls relented and collapsed in a pile on top of him, where the four friends laughed hysterically until the tears rolled down their cheeks and their stomachs hurt.

After several minutes of sweet, cleansing, gut-busting laughter, they lay back and looked at the stained acoustic-tile ceiling.

"You know, Kenzie," started Emily, after everyone had finally caught their breath. "Since you're close personal friends with Billy Weber…"

Kenzie waited, wondering what special fan request was forthcoming.

"...maybe you can get him to buy us a new ceiling. This is *awful*."

Kenzie burst out laughing. At that moment, she felt happier and more free than she had since she'd first come to PCU. Or maybe since she had in her whole life.

"Yeah, Kenzie..." chimed in Cooper. "Since your family's so stinking rich, maybe they'd remodel the whole suite for us!"

"Hey, I bought three LightSong CDs this year," said Ryan. "You think your old man could at least spring for a new couch? That old green thing looks like bad guacamole. Smells like it, too."

"Only when you're on it, Ry," Kenzie retorted. She looked at the ceiling and grinned, anticipating Ryan's tickle-fight revenge.

Everything's going to be all right. Everything's going to be just fine.

12

A t exactly eight o'clock the next morning, Kenzie's radio alarm went off, and she was awakened to the local station that played "the best hits of the Sixties and Seventies."

"Since my baby left me," the radio blared. "I found a new place to dwell/Down at the end of Lonely Street, at Heartbreak Hotel..." It was an Elvis song, one her dad had played on years before Kenzie was born. She smiled and yawned, rubbed her eyes, and waited to hear Dad's guitar solo before reaching over to turn the radio down.

I have to admit, that's pretty cool. How many kids at PCU can say their dad played with Elvis? N-O-N-E. Zip. Zero. Zilch. Nada. Just li'l ol' me...Hmm...I need to learn that guitar solo myself.

As Kenzie's eyes adjusted to the morning, she rolled over and looked out the small window. It was raining. Big surprise. This was Seattle, after all. What did she expect? But it was getting a little old.

Kenzie rolled out of bed, stretched, and headed for the bathroom. She'd gotten only six hours of sleep after her emotionally draining night. But it would be worth it, if her plan came off without a hitch.

Catching a view of herself in the full-length mirror on the back of her bedroom door, she surveyed the situation: plaid flannel nightgown, long-john bottoms, and too-big cotton socks. Her eyes were squinty, her face was creased by an obviously sound sleep, and her chestnut hair was falling every which way out of the "scrunchie" ponytail on top of her head, a la "Pebbles Flintstone."

"What a babe," she said to her reflection. "You should call Chris Gallagher right now. He'd probably write a song for you: 'She's a Dog-Faced Girl, But I Dig Her.'"

Call…oh yeah, that's why I woke up early.

Kenzie stumbled to the bathroom, where she encountered a sleepy Cooper in her thrift-shop-special, chenille bathrobe, a wardrobe item Kenzie found particularly cool.

"Mornin', Coop."

"Hey."

"Late night, wasn't it?"

Cooper yawned and checked in the mirror for zits.

Working around her suite-mate, Kenzie finished her morning bathroom routine, but decided to save the shower for later.

"Shower's all yours, Cooper. I gotta make a phone call."

Picking up the phone, she called 4-1-1 for directory assistance.

"What city?" asked the computer voice.

"Seattle."

"What listing?"

"King Plaza Hotel."

"Thank you for using Pacific Tel. Please wait."

The number Kenzie received was easy to remember, and she punched it in immediately.

"Good morning. King Plaza. How may I help you?"

"Uh, yes. Mr. Taylor's room, please."

Kenzie heard the operator's computer keyboard clicking as

she looked up the number.

"Is that Mr. O.P. Taylor?"

"Yes, thank you."

"Just one moment, I'll ring Mr. Taylor's room for you."

A gruff, sleepy male voice answered the connection.

"H-hello?..."

Kenzie grinned. Only a handful of people knew the secret code name Billy Weber used when he stayed in hotels, and she was one of them. Billy took his code name from Sheriff Andy's young son, Opie. Billy loved *The Andy Griffith Show*, and had hours and hours of old shows on videotape in the bus. He'd even met Ron Howard, the child-actor-turned-famous-director, at the Grammy Awards last year.

"Opie...it's Aunt Bea," Kenzie cooed, in a sing-song, old-lady voice. "Time for your breakfast! You're going to be late for school!"

"Ohhh...Kenzie, you little brat. What are you doing?"

"When are y'all leaving? I wanna come see you and have breakfast. And bring a friend, if that's okay. Of course, you're buyin.'"

There was a pause on the other line, then a chuckle of awareness as Billy was waking up.

"Oh, I see. Let me guess. Your friend...what's his name, that musician guy? It's early...yeah, sure, come on over. Just give me time to shower."

"You'd better. I'm not having breakfast with a scuzbucket. How's nine? I don't have class till eleven today, and neither does my friend."

"Downstairs, at the restaurant. I hear they have great French toast. See you then?"

"We're there! Thanks, Billy. You're the best."

Kenzie raced through a shower, dressed, and knocked on

Emily's door, her hair still wrapped in a towel.

"Em? Can I come in? It's Kenzie."

"Uh, yeah, I'm awake."

Kenzie couldn't believe she was actually initiating a "good morning" visit with her suite-mate. *This feels pretty good.*

Not only was Emily awake, she was sitting at her desk in her bathrobe, her Bible and plaid-covered journal spread open in front of her.

"Oh, sorry. I didn't mean to interrupt, but—" Kenzie felt a twinge of guilt for not having the kind of disciplined devotional life that Emily did.

"Oh, that's okay! I was just reading. And writing. It was quite a day yesterday. I learned a lot, I think."

"Yeah, me too. Thanks for being so understanding, really. I know you had a right to be mad."

Emily put her hand under her chin and looked at Kenzie.

"You know, I never knew how…well, normal, you really were," she said.

"You mean insecure," Kenzie laughed.

"Well, yeah…you seem so cool and together all the time."

Kenzie took the comment as a compliment.

"Well, thanks, I guess. Now you know the real scoop, though. I'm just as much of a dweeb as anybody else. Anyhow, wanna go out for breakfast? I know a cool place. My treat, even. Dad gave me some cash and told me to have some fun. And I think it might be fun to have a really great breakfast somewhere. How 'bout it, Em? You game? Thing is, we'd have to go right away, so you'd have to hurry up and get ready. Is that cool?"

Emily tucked her robe tightly around her and smiled.

"That would be great. I'll hurry. It's raining outside, isn't it? Then I won't worry too much about my hair."

"Sure…" Kenzie hesitated, knowing that Emily would die if she didn't look great for breakfast with Billy Weber. "But it'll probably clear up. I'm going to mess with mine, anyway. You just never know who you'll see out there!" Kenzie smiled like the Cheshire cat, which made Emily pleasantly suspicious.

"Kenzie, I know it hasn't been, well, great, between us—but you don't have to buy me breakfast. Really."

"No, I want to! C'mon, it'll be fun. Besides, I need some tips on how to live with a slob roommate. I have a hunch Beth's gonna be around more often now, which is a whole other story, and with that comes—well, you know." Kenzie looked over at Cooper's side of the room, which looked like the aftermath of a thrift shop explosion.

Both girls burst out laughing. "Well, sure," said Emily. "I'll tell you how I manage it. Besides, I've been craving some good French toast. My mom makes the *best.*" Emily smiled cheerfully and headed for the bathroom.

The sound of high-powered hair dryers was soon replaced by the low roar of Kenzie's Jeep Cherokee pulling out of the dorm lot and heading toward the King Plaza.

"That was record time for me; I don't know about you, Em. Hair, makeup, everything." Despite only getting six hours of sleep, Kenzie had to work hard not to grin like a big goofball.

Emily flicked the windshield sun visor down for a look in the lighted mirror. "Not bad, considering! I think we did pretty well, myself. As a matter of fact, I think we're ready to run into any guy we know at PCU. Not mentioning any names or anything, Kenzie."

"You never know, Em…but I have to admit, that Southern girl "lipstick and earrings" thing comes in handy. 'Never leave the house without at least wearing lipstick and earrings.' That's what Mom and all my aunts say." Kenzie waited for the usual response. Whenever she mentioned makeup to a West Coast girl, they always said the same thing.

Sure enough, Emily delivered. "You really don't need to wear makeup, Kenzie! You look great without it…" Silently, Kenzie finished Emily's sentence along with her: "…you're a natural beauty."

Emily looked around as they approached the hotel. "Where are we going, anyway? I don't think I've ever been around here," she said, peering at the downtown buildings near the King Plaza.

Kenzie nosed the Jeep onto the sweeping drive in front of the hotel and stopped in front of the valet parking post. With a quick, fluid motion, she put the car in park, set the brake, and left the keys dangling in the ignition.

"C'mon, Em. They'll park it for us." Kenzie accepted a numbered ticket from the valet, who was wearing khaki pants, a white Central Parking shirt, and a black rain parka.

"Wow! Breakfast at a hotel! I've only done this once before, at a youth group convention. Isn't this expensive?"

Kenzie shook her head. "Don't worry about it, Em. Remember, Dad gave me cash and told me to have fun."

As she and Emily hurried into the lobby of the hotel out of the cold, gray drizzle, Kenzie felt a rush of good feeling, knowing that what was about to take place would thrill her suite-mate.

Two nights before, this act would have been motivated by a need to absolve herself of guilt. This morning it felt pure, and Kenzie was thankful. Her prayers had been answered.

Kenzie glanced around the busy lobby and found the brass sign that read "King's Table." The hotel planners were making a play for the arena's clientele, that much was obvious. To Kenzie, though, the restaurant's name summoned images of seventeenth-century English crown banquets in great, velvet-draped halls.

It had the same effect on Emily. "'King's Table!' Are we going to have stuffed pheasant on silver trays? Really, Kenzie, French toast is fine for me!"

At the hostess stand, Kenzie gave the room a quick once-over. *No Billy yet. Rats. He's running late.*

"Two for breakfast?" A matronly hostess dressed in a maroon hotel-garb pantsuit picked up two oversized menus and gestured toward the dining room.

"Yes, that would be fine, thank you. A booth, if you can, please." Kenzie handled restaurant etiquette as easily as breathing, and she knew her way around a hotel.

The two coeds slid into opposite sides of a comfortable booth.

"Ooh, this is so fancy!" Emily said, staring at the white, starched tablecloth. "Are you sure your dad gave you enough money for this? Don't you want to spend it doing something else? I feel bad."

Kenzie picked up a teaspoon and tapped it rhythmically on the table near Emily's water glass. "Em, don't worry about it! It took me months to own up to being from a rich family, so just enjoy it, okay? I'm sorry—I didn't mean that the way it sounded."

Emily picked up her long-stemmed water glass, sipped, and smiled sweetly. "No offense taken, dear suite-mate. It's just different, that's all. I think it's great how you don't act like a rich kid. I mean, look at your car! It's nice and everything, but it's not brand new, and I guess you could…" Emily paused, wondering if she were now offending Kenzie.

"Okay," said Kenzie. "Let's just get this out of the way. I won't be offended by the rich-kid comments if you won't. Deal?"

"Deal." Emily look relieved.

"So, could I drive anything I wanted? Yeah. I could. But I don't want to. I went to high school with a bunch of rich, preppy kids who got new BMWs and Range Rovers on their sixteenth birthdays. Not that I'm *not* a rich, preppy kid…" Kenzie demurred, seeing the amused expression on Emily's face. "But my family has always been very careful about not flaunting what we have materially. Dad's family didn't have a lot of money growing up, and my mom's family was comfortable, not super-wealthy. Actually, I'm surprised Mom and Dad didn't just go hog-wild when LightSong took off."

"Why didn't they?" asked Emily. "I think if I made millions of dollars I'd be tempted to buy lots of things, although it would be fun to be able to give away money to people who needed it."

"Bingo—you've got it, Em. Mom and Dad get a kick out of helping people, and organizations, and missions. That's why Dad and Mom are both so involved with World Vision and Young Life. They give a lot of money away, but they also give their time. That's just what they decided to do, early on. My folks do have their extravagances though. You ought to see my dad on vacation!"

"That must be fun!" Emily visibly sparkled at the thought of unlimited funds for entertainment.

"Yeah, I have to admit, it is. My favorite place, though, is still our cabin in East Tennessee, in the Smoky Mountains—that's been in the Dawson family a long time. It's rustic!"

"I guess you don't have white linen tablecloths there, huh?"

"Not hardly! That one barely has plumbing!"

"With four girls? That must be a challenge!"

"Yeah, we have to take turns. It gets especially bad when we're all on the same—oh, hi, Billy!"

Billy Weber, his hair still damp from the shower, slid unannounced into the booth next to Kenzie, greeting her with a quick side-arm hug.

"Hello—Emily, right? Glad you could join us! Oh, *this* friend, Kenz. I guess I was expecting the musician guy, but this is great! Glad you could join us."

Emily looked like a deer caught in the headlights. Kenzie's chattiest suite-mate was at a loss for words in the wake of such a spectacular surprise. And she completely missed the reference to Chris, which, under normal circumstances, she would have pounced upon.

"Uh, uh…well, uh, hi, Billy! I…I…I didn't know. Oh, gosh, Kenzie! You tricked me!"

Kenzie broke into a broad, cheeky grin. She and Billy exchanged conspiratorial glances and slapped a high-five.

"HA! Not bad, huh? But I wasn't lying. My dad really did give me some cash, but I told Billy he was paying. Heck, he owes you, Em. You bought a ticket and a T-shirt—plus all those CDs, and tour books, and that jacket."

"Kenzie, stop it!" Emily protested weakly, enjoying the ribbing. "Okay, well, Billy, that's really nice. But aren't you tired from last night? I'm exhausted and all I did was listen and clap!"

"And scream." Kenzie couldn't help kidding her suite-mate, who was still flushed from the excitement of the surprise.

"Well, of course! Didn't you, Kenzie?"

"No, we don't scream backstage. We're way too cool." Kenzie's tone was sufficiently self-mocking for Emily to catch the joke.

"I left a note for Jack to come down when he gets up. He was still crashed when you called," Billy said to Kenzie.

Kenzie looked across the table. "Em, are you wondering why Billy would have a roommate, when he can obviously afford to have his own suite?"

Emily looked surprised at the question. "Well, no, not at all, actually."

"No one cares, Kenzie," Billy said with a smile. "I'll explain it, though, if you want me to. But first, have you girls ordered yet? It's on me. It's the least I can do, Emily. I think I'm in debt to you about a hundred bucks, or so Kenzie says—and don't think I don't appreciate it, either." Billy flashed his famous smile at Emily, and Kenzie admired her for not melting into the linen.

"No, but here comes our waiter, finally." Kenzie laid the Dawson charm on thick when the server arrived. "Good morning, sir! How's your French toast today? My friend here says no one can beat her mother's, but I say you can give her mom a run for her money. What do you think?"

The waiter was a clean-cut fellow who looked like he might be a grad student. He warmed to the Dawson charm, as did everyone else. It was always a sure thing, especially in places where a Southern accent was out of the ordinary.

"As a matter of fact, we're famous for our French toast. The chef uses orange peel and real vanilla in the batter, and the bread is sourdough—from the bakery at Pike Place. I eat it at least twice a week myself. But then, I've never had your mother's." He turned and smiled at Emily, who smiled right back.

Well, you don't have to be Southern to be charming, obviously, thought Kenzie. She noticed that Emily "batted her eyes just right," the way Grandmimi Chalmers says you catch a man. *Em! Bein' a flirt! You go, girl...*

"French toast, then, since you recommend it, with bacon. And a small orange juice, please?"

"Get a large, Em! Extra large! Billy's payin', remember? Soak him for all he's worth." Kenzie laughed, loving every minute of the day so far.

"I'll bring a pitcher for you all to share," said the cute waiter. "It's fresh squeezed. You'll love it."

Geez, thought Kenzie. *Is this guy Mr. Perfect, or what? Looks like Emily sure likes it.*

Kenzie and Billy went for the famed French toast as well. They also ordered up a platter of fresh fruit for starters, and a side of smoked salmon with toast wedges.

"Hey, we're in Seattle," said Kenzie. "You gotta have salmon, Billy. Especially since it's on your credit card."

"Yeah, yeah…hey, there's Jack!" Billy spotted his road manager at the hostess station and flagged him down. "Colton! Bro! Over here!" Jack strode purposefully over to the table and asked Emily if he could sit next to her.

"Sure…oh, I'm Emily Stewart, Kenzie's suite-mate."

"Jack Colton, Kenzie's ex-babysitter."

Kenzie blushed, though she'd heard this stuff a hundred times. She made a face to let them know she was through discussing it.

"Yeah, those were the days, weren't they, guys? Can we change the subject?"

"Oh, yeah…Jack, I was just about to explain to Emily here why I don't get my own suite on the road."

"We have to watch him, Emily," Jack deadpanned.

"Yeah, I've been known to trash a hotel or two," said Billy, playing along with the joke. "Those bad drug flashbacks, from my old rock-and-roll days, you know. Kind of embarrassing for the Christian music community, see."

"Yeah, one more trashed hotel, and it's good-bye, Billy Graham Crusade," said Jack.

"Okay, you guys, cut it out!" Emily was gasping for breath from laughing at their well-rehearsed patter. "My stomach hurts!"

"Well, we can't have that," said Billy. "You've got French toast to eat. By the way, Emily, I think maybe our waiter was flirting with you."

"Duuuhhh! Like it's not obvious, Weber," said Kenzie.

"Well, you know…it takes us guys a while to figure this stuff out."

"Which goes back to the real reason why Billy doesn't have his own suite, Em," Kenzie offered.

"This is embarrassing for me, Em," said Billy, taking a swig from Kenzie's water glass and munching an ice cube. "Just so you know. But it's a good reason; I just don't like to talk about it."

"Let me guess—you guys share a suite so you stay out of trouble, right, Billy? All those crazed fans wanting to throw themselves at you?"

"*Em!*" Kenzie was genuinely shocked at her suite-mate's candid question.

"What? It makes sense. Anyway, I think taking precautions is a wise thing to do."

"The thing is, Em, Billy's been doing this all along, ever since he started touring," explained Kenzie.

"You can't be too careful," added Billy. "I know what the Bible says about 'avoiding the appearance of evil', and you just have to go to great lengths to make sure people know where you're coming from. In fact, I wouldn't have had breakfast alone even with Kenzie, if you can believe that."

"*As if*…yuck, gross!" Kenzie slipped easily into the "kid sister" role with Billy, after years of friendship.

"Gee, thanks. But, seriously, Emily—think of the most famous Christian in the world, besides the Pope, of course. And Mother Teresa."

"Billy Graham?"

"Right. In all of his years of public ministry, he's never had one whiff of scandal around him. And you know why? Because a long time ago, back in the early days of his ministry, he and his staff made a pledge—the Modesto Manifesto, it was called—and since then, he has made it a point to always travel with a male staff member. He doesn't even have lunch with a woman alone, except his wife or daughters. Won't even get into an elevator with a woman by himself," said Billy, with admiration in his voice.

"We're not quite that strict with our Billy," Jack interjected. "But Billy Graham's living proof that being careful pays off. That's why Weber never stays in a room by himself," he said. "Unfortunately, Billy—Weber, that is—snores something awful. Sounds like an army helicopter. That's why we send his wife out on tour as often as possible, to spread the misery around."

Everyone laughed, and Kenzie couldn't help but feel that her worlds had finally come together. Emily was calmly enjoying the presence of Billy Weber. Billy seemed comfortable, and so was Kenzie. *Too bad Dad had to leave so early.*

The waiter reappeared, bearing a pitcher of orange juice and the tray of fruit. He poured the juice as if it were French champagne, starting with Emily's glass, which didn't escape Emily's notice. Nor Kenzie's.

"I'll have your salmon right up," he said. Kenzie spied his name tag, and noticed Emily doing the same. *David Rolf. Emily and David. David and Emily. Emily Rolf.* Kenzie played the "what if" game, marrying off Emily to a total stranger before they were even formally introduced. *Chris and Kenzie Gallagher. If guys knew we did this, they'd die.*

"And your French toast isn't far behind," he said to Emily. "Trust me; it's worth the wait."

Billy and Jack began scarfing up the fresh fruit, spearing hunks of pineapple and cantaloupe, banana chunks, kiwi slices, and enormous, picture-perfect strawberries. "How they get berries like this in February is beyond me," said Billy.

"Who cares where they get 'em—they're great, huh?" said Kenzie.

Emily hadn't touched the fruit plate, leaving the details of its demise to the men and her always-hungry suite-mate.

"So, Emily…this waiter seems kind of interested in you," said Billy. "What do you think? Or do you have a boyfriend at PCU? Kenzie tells me the pickin's are slim—these West Coast guys are too organic for her, which makes me wonder why she came out here in the first place."

"I did *not* say that! I like the rugged, Northwest kind of look. Flannel shirts and all that." Kenzie folded her arms across her chest.

"What about this Chris guy? I thought that's who you were bringing to breakfast—although it's great that you came, Emily."

"Chris? You know about Chris? Kenzie, why didn't you ask him to come? Don't you think he would have loved this?" Emily was truly curious about this.

"Uh, we can talk about me any time. Why don't you tell Billy what you thought about his show?" Kenzie suggested.

"Well, I—" Suddenly, Emily appeared to realize that she was actually at breakfast with her idol, Billy Weber. She cleared her throat nervously.

"That's right. How *did* you like the concert, Emily?" Jack was always eager to gauge the reaction of Billy's audience. "Did you like the opening acts?"

"Oh, yes!" Emily brightened at Jack's genuine interest. "They were great. Of course, I've heard them on the radio a lot, but they were even better live. I'm planning to get both of their CDs, next time I have some spare cash."

"Hey, no problem. We'll get you a couple. In fact, I might have one in my briefcase—" Jack rifled through his soft-sided leather attaché. "Yep, here's one," he said, flipping the CD onto the table. "And, good! Here's the other one—enjoy! Do you have Billy's latest? I've got one of those in here, too."

"Oh, of course! I bought it the first day it was out—I had it on advance order from our Christian bookstore."

"Great. Well, here's one for a friend or something. They're just taking up room in my briefcase." Jack smiled at Billy, who didn't even notice the slam.

"Oh, thank you!" Emily said. To her surprise, Kenzie realized that Emily was quite composed, not at all out of control.

"Hey, guys, did you know that Emily does the Christian radio show on our campus station? She's getting pretty good. And she promoted the heck out of your show, Billy." Kenzie surprised herself, and Emily, too, with her open display of support for Emily's Christian music endeavors.

"Well, I guess I'll have to call in and do an interview next time, huh?" said Billy. "Wait; I have a better idea!" Suddenly, he hopped up from the table and jogged out of the restaurant.

"He's probably going to get his portable DAT out of his room," said Jack.

"DAT? What's that?"

Kenzie roared at Emily's accidental rhyme. "Good one, Em! DAT stands for digital audio tape. It's a superior mode of tape recording, but you have to have a special machine to record and play back on. Billy's probably going to do a station ID for you. Then somebody at the station can dub it down, and you can play it on your show."

"You just said a lot of things I don't understand." Emily looked dismayed. "I'm new at this you know. Maybe Ethan can help?"

"Or Chris. He's probably got a DAT himself, I'll bet." Kenzie smiled shyly at the thought.

"Well, *you* ask him, Kenzie," said Emily. "It's about time you got this show on the road!"

"That's exactly what Allie said, Em! Did you get that from her?"

"No, I just think it's true! If you like someone, you just have to let them know somehow. Right, guys?" Emily looked up at a breathless Billy, who'd just arrived at the table, bearing the DAT. It looked to her like a fancy Walkman, except for the attached microphone.

"Sure, right, whatever you said. Okay, here it is. It's quiet enough in here to do this, so let's go! What's the name of your radio station?"

Kenzie gazed affectionately at her old friend, feeling impressed by his willingness to go the extra mile for Emily. *What a guy. Of course, it's being married to Susan that's made him this thoughtful. She trained him right. And his mama. He is a Southern boy, after all.*

After clearing off a spot on the table, Billy fired up the DAT and started recording Emily's station IDs.

"Hi, this is Billy Weber, and you're listening to the Christian music show with Emily Stewart on 91 Rock, WPCU." Emily was transfixed, almost unable to comprehend her good fortune.

Billy tried another, and another, to make sure. "Hi, this is Billy Weber. Tune in Thursday nights at 7:00 for the best in Christian music with Emily Stewart on 91 Rock, WPCU."

"Will that work for you?" Billy popped the tape out and handed it to a delighted Emily.

"Wow. Are the guys at the radio station ever going to be impressed! Thank you so much!"

"Sure. Glad to do it. Hey, if you ever need any more CDs, call—Kenzie's dad!" Billy broke into a laugh at his own joke.

"Well, this has been great, but we need to get going, Billy," Jack prodded. "You've got to catch the bus to Vancouver, you know."

"Vancouver. Wish I could go," said Kenzie. "My favorite city in the world…besides San Francisco…Dublin…London…and Nashville, of course! You're going to eat at Sala Thai, my favorite, aren't you? Have the chili-garlic shrimp for me."

The waiter appeared with the check and waited while Billy signed the receipt and calculated a hefty tip. "Thank you, sir…" Looking both professional and handsome in his starched apron and bow tie he hesitated, then asked, "Mr. Weber? I didn't want to disturb your breakfast, but I wanted to tell you that I really enjoyed your concert last night."

Kenzie and Emily stared at each other as though he'd just said he was the true heir to the British crown.

13

A ctually," said the waiter, "I took my sister for her birthday—she's been a big fan of yours for a long time. She even has your very first album."

"She has *Billy Weber: Lost And Found?* With the dorky cover? Wow!" Jack was incredulous. "That's a collector's item, you know. Hey, how about that picture of Billy, huh? Bad Hair Year for him. I know LightSong would love to track those down and burn 'em."

"Well, I'm sure my sister wouldn't give it up; she still plays it all the time. Excuse me, Mr. Weber?"

"Billy. Call me Billy."

"Thank you. Listen, I hate to do this, but would you mind signing something for her? She'd be thrilled out of her mind."

"Sure…how about a tour book? I'm sure Jack has one of those in his amazing briefcase."

"No," said Jack, fishing. "But, here's an itinerary. Kind of an authentic tour thing. Sign away, Young William."

Billy wrote a note and handed it to the smiling waiter.

"Thank you so much! I hope I didn't disturb you. But I did enjoy the show, and I guess I'll have to borrow my sister's CDs and listen some more."

"Wait! Here's one!" Emily blushed at her impulsive gift, which she practically slammed on the table in front of David.

"Oh, no, I couldn't...I'm sorry, I didn't catch your name..."

"Emily! Emily Stewart!" Kenzie practically yelled it, eager to get things rolling between her suite-mate and this guy. *It's been a tough year for Em, romantically speaking.* "Sorry. And I'm Kenzie Dawson."

"Emily? Great name. I love Emily Dickinson, the poet. Oh, by the way, I'm David Rolf. Nice to meet you both," he said, finally acknowledging Kenzie with a nod in her direction. "Do you go to U-Dub?"

"No, PCU," said Emily. "We're both freshm— "

"Fresh on campus! New this year." Kenzie interrupted her suite-mate's introduction, afraid of jinxing Emily's chances with this guy by revealing her tender age. "Are you in grad school at U-Dub?"

"No, actually, I'm at PCU, too. Senior. English major."

Billy and Jack stood up and shook hands with David, indicating that it was time for them to leave. "Nice to meet you. I guess we gotta go—but, hey! Glad we could introduce you kids, since you go to the same school and everything."

The impossible had occurred. Emily Stewart, Billy Weber's most rabid fan, barely noticed his presence, let alone his imminent departure.

"Emily?" Billy tried to catch her attention. "Glad you could join us."

"Oh! Billy! Yes, thank you so much! It was great. Really great. I mean, I never imagined—who would have thought—"

"You're welcome. Thanks again for coming last night. Have a good semester, and keep our girl Kenzie out of trouble, okay? Or at least out of jail."

Billy and Jack laughed and walked with Kenzie out into the

154

lobby, leaving Emily and David to their moon-eyed chat.

"Good grief," laughed Kenzie. "Was that totally sickening or what? Like magnets, those two. Did he even notice us? Did he have any other tables? I think you just lost your "Coolest Guy In The World" status, Weber. And to a waiter, no less. He should have left *you* a big tip!"

"Oh well—you win some, you lose some," said Billy. "I'm just glad I could bring the happy couple together. Speaking of which—what are you doin' about this musician guy, huh, Kenz? I think you oughta fake like you want guitar lessons from him. Then when he finds out how good you are, y'all can hit the road as a duo and make beautiful music together." Billy winked, and Kenzie pretended to stick her finger down her throat, making gagging sounds.

"You sound just like Dad with that duo thing. Yeah, right. I don't want to blow him away on guitar and embarrass the guy, Billy! Those fragile male egos, you know," she teased.

"Yeah, I know…Susan reminds me of that all the time—oh! I almost forgot something!" Billy raced to the front desk, procured a package from behind the counter, and ran back to where Kenzie had been joined by a glowing Emily.

"I almost forgot to give you these. From Susan. Chocolate chip cookies for you, Kenz. But she'd better share them with suite-mates, right, Emily?"

Emily shot Kenzie an "I'm going to kill you" look, remembering the Unfortunate Cookie Mailing Incident and wondering if Kenzie had ratted on her.

"Of course I'll share!" Kenzie grabbed the brown paper package and handed it to Emily. "We're not the cookie-baking types in our suite. Are we, Em?" said Kenzie, with a theatrical wink.

"Let's put it this way—we're always happy to get care packages from home," said Emily, grinning thankfully at Kenzie.

"Now you guys have a good trip, and a great tour! We're praying for you."

She's so good about that, thought Kenzie. *I always forget to pray for Billy. Guess I wouldn't mind if some of Em's habits rubbed off on me.*

After the good-byes, the girls headed back to PCU for their late-morning classes, Emily bubbling nonstop about her "incredibly, unbelievably awesome" morning and clutching her treasures in her hand: the tape of Billy's promotions for the radio show, the CDs of the opening acts, and a King's Table matchbook, inscribed with David Rolf's phone number.

"Can you believe it, Kenzie?! As if it weren't enough to be totally surprised by you taking me to breakfast with Billy Weber—which was SO nice of you. Then to have totally great French toast, and all that fancy food, and to get those station promotions and to have Billy Weber buy my breakfast. And *then* to meet a cute guy from PCU, who likes Billy Weber, and—"

"And you. He likes you!" Kenzie honked the horn for emphasis and waved to a passing pedestrian as she wheeled the Jeep into the dorm parking lot.

"Do you think so?" Emily asked dreamily.

"Oh, geez, Em. He virtually ignored a huge pop star, sitting right at his table, not to mention a Fabulous Southern Babe, right in front of him. And he got your phone number, right? Hello! Em? Em? Is the caller there?"

Emily didn't answer. She just smiled at Kenzie and absent-mindedly opened the door, lost in a world populated by starched-apron waiters quoting Emily Dickinson.

14

llie, it was unbelievable. Straight out of a cheap romance
novel. I mean, 'Emily's a great name.' Give me a fat break!
Fortunately, he didn't start quoting Emily Dickinson right
there, while he was pouring coffee."

Kenzie hadn't been on the PCU campus fifteen minutes
before she'd run into Allie and started giving her the scoop on
the morning's events.

Inspired, Allie began to recite:

"There's a certain Slant of light,
 Winter afternoons—
That oppresses, like the Heft
Of Cathedral Tunes — "

"Allie, is that your American Lit assignment, or do you just
happen to have it in your head all the time? I'm assuming that's
Emily Dickinson you're spouting."

"Yes, it is, and I'm shocked you don't know it. Didn't you go
to a prep school? Besides, you Southerners have that great literary
tradition; not that Emily Dickinson was a Southerner. Poetry

should be a part of your life, though, Kenzie."

"How about 'Since my baby left me/I've found a new place to dwell/Down at the end of Lonely Street, at Heartbreak Hotel...'" Kenzie sang, in her worst Elvis impression. "Now *that's* poetry. From the Elvis period in Southern literature."

Allie hooted with laughter. "I dare you to go in to Dr. Coleman's class and do that. By the way, did you get your reading done?"

"Short stories? Faulkner, Welty, Hannah? Oops, forgot. Just kidding. Of course I did. Gotta stand up proud for the Southern literary tradition, you know. Hey, do you think Dr. Coleman would believe that my dad played the guitar solo on 'Heartbreak Hotel?'"

"Yeah, right. Then she'd make you bring him for Show and Tell."

"Hey, it could happen."

The two friends entered the ivy-covered hall, just in time to slide into chairs in Room 222 as Dr. RoseAnne Coleman closed the door behind them.

Fifty minutes of discussion on William Faulkner's Southern Gothic short story, "A Rose For Emily," served to whet their curiosity about their own Emily and her newly budded romance. When Dr. Coleman assigned a short paper for the following week, Allie and Kenzie each wrote the homework carefully in their study planners, but Allie wrote, in large block letters in her notebook, big enough for Kenzie to read: A ROSE FOR EMILY. NONE FOR YOU OR ME. WE'RE LOSERS.

After Dr. Coleman dismissed the class, the two shouldered their bookpacks and headed for lunch.

"Kenzie, you realize it's almost your birthday, don't you?"

"And Valentine's Day. Don't forget." Kenzie made a face at Allie.

"Yeah, so…what are we going to do? The sororities and fraternities are all doing stuff, but we're doing nothing. *Nada.* What a bummer. Two Fabulous Babes like us, and we're stuck without anything to do on such an incredibly romantic day."

"Yep," said Kenzie, swinging the dining hall door open. "Cooper has Ryan, Beth has what's-his-name, and now even Emily has another love interest—funny, he's another knight-in-shining-armor type. Poetry and all. Why is she such a Poet Magnet? I think it's trouble."

Allie grabbed an orange plastic tray and scooted it along the aluminum track in front of the food selections. "Chicken sandwich, please. Hold the mayo."

Kenzie peered over the stainless-steel counter to observe the cafeteria worker. "Allie, she's not holding the mayo. She's not even touching it. You told her to hold it, and she hasn't even picked it up."

"You're warped, you know that? No wonder you're going to be dateless on your birthday-slash-Valentine's Day! I think Emily's a Poet Magnet because she's got that dreamy look on her face all the time. She needs to read that creepy Faulkner story, don't you think? On the other hand, maybe she's got a good thing going. How many boys are making a play for us, huh? Unless you count Chris, who is so shy he probably doesn't dress in front of his roommate."

"Allie! You're so wrong. He's not that shy! He comes alive when he's playing music, haven't you noticed? Like at Young Life Leadership? And at The Cup? He just needs a little encouragement, that's all." Kenzie turned to the cafeteria lady and asked politely for two hot dogs and a side of fries.

"And you're going to give it to him? When? The millennium's almost over. Hey, I've got an idea! Hmmm…yep, this is too good. I'll grab a table and then we'll discuss."

"We'll 'discuss'? Okay, 'Dr.' Raju. We'll discuss."

Sticking a large cup of ice under the soft drink fountain, Kenzie filled it to the brim with foaming root beer and headed for Allie's table.

"All right, what is it? Spill the plan." Kenzie doused her hot dog with mustard and took a healthy bite.

"'Heartbreak Hotel.' Your Elvis moment inspired me. We'll have a 'Heartbreak Hotel' party, for all of us who don't have Blips on the Love Radar Screen."

"Thhahht's ghhweat!" Kenzie said through a mouthful of hot dog. The news was too good to worry about table manners.

"We can have it at your suite, since your goony-eyed suite-mates will all be on some romantic dates. Maybe they could drop by after they've done the hearts and flowers thing. I mean, it is your birthday and everything. The least they can do is pay their respects." Allie reached over and absconded with a hand-ful of Kenzie's fries.

"No, really, Allie, I couldn't possibly eat all these fries," Kenzie said sarcastically. "So, who's invited? Besides me, of course. I presume I'd be the guest of honor."

"Of course! And then Chris. And Drew, unless he scores a date somewhere. And Ethan. You know, we need to get that boy hooked up with somebody. I sorta figured he was good for Emily, but—"

"Trust me; this waiter guy with the good vocabulary is Em's type. Maybe. Then again, he could be a poetry-quoting ax mur-derer. Who knows? OK, so who else?"

"Well…" Allie paused and took a sip of her Diet Coke. "The rule should be that you can't come unless you're unattached. Romantically, I mean. Not mentally—since you're the guest of honor and everything, you'd have to be there."

Kenzie didn't even bother to roll her eyes in response.

"Continue. Will there be roses, champagne, a string quartet?"

"I don't think so. That'll be Emily's date with Poetry Boy. We'll have….Elvis! That's it! Everybody can come dressed as inhabitants of 'Heartbreak Hotel'! We'll get Drew to dress up like Elvis, and I'll be Priscilla Presley! Maybe we can raid the Young Life skit closet and get a wig!" Allie's party wheels were turning.

"Hey, Cooper's got all that funky vintage stuff, somewhere in that wreck of a room! I'll bet she's got a cool Sixties dress, or maybe some white go-go boots for you, Al. But you don't need a wig, you know. With that hair, all you need is some good ol' Southern beauty parlor hair teasing and some Aqua-Net hair spray. We can have you lookin' like Elvis's child bride in a heartbeat."

"Heartbreak, you mean." Allie and Kenzie raised their hands for a spontaneous high-five across the table.

"This'll be great, Allie. A fine idea. Hey, if I know my mom, she'll send me a little money for a party, so we can order a cake and everything. And pizza, of course. Maybe score some champagne from somewhere, too."

"Are you nuts? If we drink at this party, Eve Garrett'll hear about it, and there goes our chances to be Young Life leaders in North Seattle next year."

"That's not true…but I get the point. Well, I don't even like champagne, to tell you the truth. I had some at my sister's wedding and those little bubbles went right to my head. Mom had to come into my bathroom that night and hold a cold cloth to my forehead while I—"

"Let me guess: Kenzie Dawson, Olympic Hurler, calling Ralph on the big white telephone. You're a case, you know that?"

"It felt like I'd had a case of champagne. But it wasn't even a whole glass. Of course, I'd been up late the night before, and I'd been too nervous and excited to eat that whole day—being a bridesmaid is serious, you know."

"Oh! Well, I wouldn't know. But you can coach me, when I'm one in your wedding. Yours and Chris's."

"Mmffmff!" Mid-chew, Kenzie could only make noise in protest to Allie's teasing.

"Whatever happened to your Southern belle manners, Mary Mackenzie? Ah'm appalled. And so's your muthah," Allie said, in a halfway decent Southern accent.

Kenzie finished chewing, swallowed, and washed the remains of her lunch down with the last of her root beer. "Let's get this 'Heartbreak Hotel' thing moving. I don't have class till three—why don't we drive over to the Young Life office and scope out the skit closet? Then maybe we can talk to Eve, too. I never did mention that weirdo dream to her, you know."

"You've got a lot of catching up to do. Like how the whole Billy thing went, and with your dad, and Emily—you don't seem so uptight about her anymore."

"It's a long story, Allie. But a good one. I think God's been listening to these desperate prayers of mine." Kenzie shook her head and chuckled as the two got up and bused their tables.

Outside the PCU student union, not even the gray skies and freezing drizzle could dampen the spirits of the two party planners. On the way to Young Life's North Seattle office near the University of Washington's Fraternity Row, Kenzie and Allie gabbed, laughed, and commiserated about their single, unattached condition, all the while making plans for the "Heartbreak Hotel" extravaganza.

"I think you and Drew should start off by crashing Leadership as Elvis and Priscilla," said Kenzie. "I could be your chauffeur—too bad we don't have a big ol' Cadillac with fins.

Now *that* would be cool! Maybe Eve knows somebody—she knows everybody."

"Hey, maybe you and Chris could work up a couple of Elvis tunes to play at Leadership next week! Then Drew and I could come as Elvis and Priscilla, and we could invite some Young Life people to the party later."

"Are you nuts? Invite 100 U-Dub people to a teensy PCU party in my suite? We'd be dead meat with the campus police." Kenzie grimaced, then smiled at the thought of making this a huge occasion.

"Okay, so maybe we could just invite a few of the PCU people from Young Life."

"Sounds cool," said Kenzie, deftly negotiating a parallel parking job near the Young Life office. "Hey, Eve's car is here. Gotta love it."

The two friends pulled their parka hoods over their heads against the cold drizzle. Remarkably, neither girl was wearing a baseball cap.

"Hey, Eve! Are the babies here?" Kenzie walked right past Eve's desk and into another office, where Eve sometimes kept her toddlers during work hours.

"Hi, girls! I'm so glad to see you. No one comes to see me anymore," said Eve, with a wry smile. "Just the kids. That's okay. I'm secure."

Allie ran to the back office and scooped up McCall, a petite two-year-old with white-blond hair. "We can't help it if you have the cutest kids in the world!" she exclaimed, wrapping McCall in a big hug.

"Second cutest," said Kenzie, who'd found Camden, the all-boy four-year-old who was too busy playing trucks to return Kenzie's affection. "My nieces and nephews are first cutest. You understand."

Eve Garrett, a svelte, red-headed former college athlete, perched on the edge of her industrial-looking metal desk. Behind her, two huge bulletin boards bore hundreds of photos of kids: her own, the high schoolers in North Seattle's Young Life clubs, and the college kids and young adults who worked with them as Young Life volunteers. In every snapshot, young faces radiated with life, energy, and laughter. Kenzie and Allie loved to gaze at the bulletin boards. Secretly, they were always looking for their own pictures: evidence that they were part of the wild, happy group of adults committed to sharing their faith with teenagers not much younger than themselves.

"So, what are you two up to now? You look like you're cruising for trouble."

"It's Kenzie's birthday on Valentine's Day, and we're going to have a 'Heartbreak Hotel' party for all the losers who don't have dates: namely, ourselves." They laughed.

"I never had a date on Valentine's Day, either...just so you feel better," Eve said. "Until Doug came along, that is. We'd been dating seriously for about four months, but when Valentine's came around, we did a 'Sleepless in Seattle' thing: took separate cars and met at the top of the Space Needle. We acted like we'd never seen each other before and were meeting for the first time, just to fake people out. Dorky, I know. But it was a blast."

"That's so cool! Okay, so you're just the person to help us out on this," Allie exclaimed. "We want to dress Drew and me up as Elvis and Priscilla—maybe crash Leadership, if that's OK with you, then go back to Kenzie's suite for our own party. But we need some Sixties stuff. You don't by any chance know someone with an old Cadillac, do you?" Allie looked hopeful.

"Let's see...maybe...oh! I've got just the thing." Eve went to a huge closet at the back of the office and rummaged through a big box. As she found them, she handed her discoveries to Allie. "Here are some funky sunglasses...fishnet pantyhose... and...wait, here they are! Ta-da!" Triumphantly, Eve held up a pair of white go-go boots, then peered in to check the size.

"Size nines, Allie. Kind of big, huh? Stuff tissue in there, you'll be fine. Now, am I invited to this soiree, or does being married with two children disqualify me?" Eve's expression let the girls know she wasn't serious about an invitation.

"You and Doug could be chaperones." Kenzie snickered. "Maybe Allie'll invite you to her wedding with Drew."

"As *if.*" Allie set the Priscilla Presley treasures down in a chair, and looked thoughtfully at Kenzie. "Hey, don't you think you should tell Eve about...you know, Chris? And the dream and everything?"

Kenzie stood up, towering over Camden and his toys.

"Probably...Eve, do you have a minute? You just wouldn't believe what's been going on with me lately."

Kenzie settled down by Eve's side, and her friend listened intently, averting her focus only to attend to her toddlers' needs.

"It sounds like you've been carrying a lot of guilt about several different things," Eve finally said. "Sounds like it's hard for you to forgive yourself, even when you know God's forgiven you. I know; I've been there, and in worse places than you."

"Really?" Kenzie was surprised, but when she thought about it, Eve seemed like the kind who might have made a mistake or two herself.

"Cut yourself some grace. Then spend some time deciding how you'll make different choices next time you're dating somebody. Like Chris, maybe?" Even Eve couldn't resist some gentle joshing.

Forty-five minutes later, Kenzie and Allie left the Young Life office, bearing party clothes and pensive expressions.

"Is Eve the wisest woman in the world, or what?" Kenzie mused. "I love that: 'Cut yourself some grace.' Wow."

"I know—don't you just kind of hate that she nails you with those deep insights like that? I mean, you hate it and love it at the same time. It's like she can see inside your soul or something."

"Well, Allie, sounds like what you told me about the dream wasn't far off. That Dylan stuff—you know, being afraid to get in a dating relationship with another musician, because I got too swept up in the last one? Eve totally agreed with you about that. Wow."

All the way home, Kenzie and Allie marveled at Eve's wisdom, and her balance of encouragement and gentle caution.

"I was pretty impressed with that 'safety valve' thing. You know, what she said about how you need to be careful: like not praying with a guy, in his car, in the dark. It made sense, the way she explained spiritual intimacy can move naturally into physical intimacy if you're not careful. She doesn't pull any punches, does she?"

"That's for sure. What's really great, though, is how she's so honest about her own struggles—what she went through when she was our age, and what she goes through even now. That's so cool. And she nailed you, in a nice way, Kenz, about relaxing in the gifts God's given you. Like your family, and—what'd she say?—'Leaning into' your musical talents?"

"Yeah." Kenzie nodded. "And, boy, she really hammered me about Chris!"

"Oh, yeah…that if you don't start opening up to him, she's going to make you start leading songs with him at Leadership?"

"It could happen. Actually, it might be kinda fun. I miss playing Young Life songs. And to be really honest, Allie? OK, this sounds totally dorky, but…Chris plays a lot like I do. We really *could* make beautiful music together."

Allie screamed with delight. "Wooooo!!!"

"If you *ever* repeat that to *anyone*, I'll *kill* you. I'm not *kidding*, Al!" Kenzie's fair skin blushed deep crimson.

"Okay, put your money where your mouth is. If you don't at least talk to him about music at Leadership this weekend, your party's off. Forget it. I'm not planning a party for a permanent loser, only a temporary one. Got that?"

"I got it. I'll ask him about his guitar or something. Okay?"

Well, this is it, thought Kenzie. *It's half over, anyway, all this coming clean about who I really am. Now I have to play guitar in front of Chris, God and everybody.*

I guess I should change my strings…

15

Late the following night, while she was alone in her room, Kenzie pulled a dusty, black guitar case out of her closet, laid it on the bed, and ceremoniously unfastened the latches. Inside, gleaming in its gold velvet resting place, lay a 1940 Martin—looking forlorn and sad, Kenzie thought.

She pulled it from its close fitting case and instantly smelled the familiar, musty odor of stale metal strings, tarnished by the sweat and oil of players' hands—hers, and her daddy's before her, and others before him. As a member in good standing, Johnny Dawson had bought the instrument from a fellow picker from the Grand Ole Opry. Johnny was required to perform a certain number of times a year, with his brother, Floyd. Kenzie remembered hearing the tapes of old shows, in which they had been introduced by Mr. Roy Acuff, the "King of Country Music."

"Let's give a great big Grand Ole Opry welcome to Johnny and Floyd Dawson—The Little Dawson Boys!"

Kenzie caught a tear from the corner of her eye, and it surprised her. *Mr. Acuff is gone now, but he sure did love my dad. And*

Miss Minnie's gone now, too.

Kenzie's thoughts wandered home, to Nashville, to the stage of the venerable old Ryman Auditorium, where the Grand Ole Opry radio show was performed for many years. Her dad had played on the old stage, and the new one, after the Opry moved out to the new Opryland complex in the Seventies. Kenzie had met Roy Acuff and Minnie Pearl, and her dad had made her play "The Wildwood Flower" for them. Both were duly impressed, or just polite. And it was *this* guitar she'd played that tune on. It had seemed bigger than her, back then. Now, it fit just right as she cradled it under her arms.

She took a flat pick from the guitar case and formed a G chord. One strum told her it was way past time to change the strings. Even so, she marveled at the resonance. *Nothing like a pre-war Martin,* she thought. *So mellow. Too mellow for the stage, though.*

She thought about Gruhn Guitars on Nashville's famed Lower Broadway. As she thought about Gruhn, her father, Mr. Acuff, and Elvis—the King of Rock and Roll—Kenzie was struck once again by the fact that her dad had at one time been considered one of the best musicians in Nashville. He'd stopped recording long ago, in favor of developing young Christian artists. The move had made him a bundle, to be sure; the fact that Kenzie's tuition was paid effortlessly with one check was proof of that. But Kenzie wondered if her dad ever missed just picking up the guitar and sitting in with Mr. Acuff's Smoky Mountain Boys, taking Charlie Collins' guitar flat-picking solo on the famous "Wabash Cannonball," or strapping on his classic old Fender Telecaster and ripping into a rockabilly riff, like he did during those years of touring with Elvis.

Now that's where we could have gotten an old Cadillac. Elvis gave one to Dad years ago, and he went and sold it when he started

LightSong. Oh, well. At least he's got a picture of it.

Kenzie was getting a mental picture of her own. In it, she was relaxed, standing on stage at the old Ryman Auditorium, in front of an old-fashioned microphone emblazoned with a big red-and-white WSM 560 sign. Next to her, on one side of the stage, was Mr. Acuff, balancing his fiddle under his chin, while the delighted crowd fanned themselves in the stifling Nashville summer heat. Next to Mr. Acuff was Miss Minnie, grinning till her eyes disappeared, wearing that funny dress and the trademark price-tagged hat. Hank Williams, Sr., stood lean and lanky in a tall cowboy hat, looking on, while a young Elvis in a pink-and-black shirt peered around the corner of the curtain, waiting politely. In the front row of the audience were Kenzie's mom and dad, looking exactly as they had when she said good-bye to them at the SEA-TAC airport last September, except that they were swatting the steamy air with WSM paper fans, having been transported to another time.

"Ladies and gentlemen," Mr. Acuff said, after taking the fiddle from under his chin. "I'm proud to introduce to you a fine pair of youngsters, all the way from Pacific Cascades University in Seattle, Washington. Now I know those folks way up there can't hear us tonight on the Grand Ole Opry, but we're sure they'll be hearing from these two younguns some other time. Will you please give a great big Grand Ole Opry welcome to Chris Gallagher and Nashville's own Kenzie Dawson…The Cascade Mountaineers!"

Tap. Tap. Tap. The hesistant knocking on Kenzie's door snapped her out of her fanciful Grand Ole Opry reverie.

"Kenzie? It's Emily. Can I come in?"

"Sure. Come in—" Emily had already opened the door before Kenzie thought to put her guitar back in its case.

"I heard music in here, and it sounded live—I wondered

who was in here with you. Oh, no one? Wha—is that *your* guitar? Was that you? It sounded like a record!"

Kenzie looked baffled.

"What do you call what you were playing?" asked Em. "Was that country? Bluegrass? It was nice. All that fancy picking. You've been at it for an hour."

Suddenly, Kenzie caught a glimpse of her fingertips. They were grooved in the centers, and blackened, like she'd been playing a guitar with old metal strings for quite a while.

"For how long, did you say?"

It was Emily's turn to look baffled. "Well, I've been hearing this for an hour or so, since I started studying."

"Wow. I kind of get lost when I play. Like I'm in another world."

"Well, that's some world! You're amazingly good! Why didn't you ever play before? We could have sold tickets and bought a new couch by now!" Emily pulled up a desk chair—the clean one, from Kenzie's side—and sat across from her.

"Uh, well...you know how I told you all that stuff about my dad, and Billy Weber, and everything? Well...this was the missing piece. I just wasn't ready to pull it out. For cryin' out loud—there was enough stuff already, don't you think?"

"Hm. Interesting, Kenzie. Do you want to know what I've been praying about for you lately?"

"You've been praying for me? Emily, I can't believe it. I don't deserve that."

"As if any of us do, Kenzie! I was just talking to God about you, that's all. Not that it's not a big deal, but...you know what I mean." Emily looked slightly embarrassed by Kenzie's comment.

"Okay. So what did he say?" Kenzie smiled, trying to shake the fogginess from her brain.

"Well, I've been praying that you would seek the truth, and that you would be open to what God had for you, in every area of your life, instead of—" She hesitated, wondering if she'd said too much.

"Instead of what?" Kenzie's question was gentle and filled with a genuine curiosity.

"Instead of…well, trying to control things. Is that hard for you, maybe?" Emily winced.

Kenzie laughed softly. "Yeah, just maybe. Looks like your prayers are being answered, Em! All over the place. So, thanks. I appreciate it. God's not finished with me yet, obviously."

Emily reached over and squeezed Kenzie's strumming arm. "Or with any of us. Kind of a relief, isn't it?"

"Yeah. So, Em? Speaking of answers to prayers—what about this cute waiter, Dave? Do you have a Valentine's date? Is he sending you mushy notes yet?"

Emily looked crestfallen. "No. He hasn't called, either. But it's only been thirty-six hours. Ryan says that's not very long in Guy Time."

"They have no clue what we go through, Em. They torture us, and they don't mean to. They're just dense, that's all."

"And Chris? Have you—"

"We're just friends, so far. I saw him at the post office today, with Allie. She let it slip that my birthday was Valentine's Day and invited him to our party, but he's got to play at The Cup that night. Maybe we'll check him out later. That's par for the course, for a 'Heartbreak Hotel' party, don't you think—when the guy you have a crush on can't even go? But you're going, right? Unless you have a date with Poetry Boy."

Emily tightened the clip on the back of her hair and smiled her perky Emily smile. "Well, I'm not holding my breath, but…it did sort of seem like he liked me, and…well, I hope I hear from him. Maybe." She hesitated. "I'm kind of gun-shy about these poetic types, since the fiasco with John."

"I understand. Believe me, I understand. I dated a musician once, and that almost cured me forever. Till I met Chris, anyway." Kenzie was enjoying the new-found comfort in talking with Emily.

"Kenzie, would you play your guitar in the living room? Cooper and Ryan are here, you know, 'studying.' They could hear you, too, but I swear we all thought it was a CD."

Kenzie rubbed her temples as though she had a headache. "Well, I don't know. I haven't played for a while, and—"

"Oh, come on, Kenz. You're great. And you need to share your talent. Staying in your room is like hiding your light under a bushel basket, like it says in the Bible."

"Are guitars in the Bible? I missed that part. I guess I should read more." Kenzie grinned and picked up her beloved Martin, on her way out to the living room. "Em, you're in that vocal group—how about if you sing something with me?"

"Sure! What do you know that we could sing together?"

"Take a wild guess." Kenzie gave Em a mischievous look.

"A Billy Weber song?"

"Forget it. No way!" laughed Kenzie, as she launched into one of his biggest hits: one she'd heard Em humming around the suite all year.

16

During the week leading up to her birthday, Kenzie Dawson discovered great joy in playing her Martin guitar on the ugly green couch, whether people were around or not. She found herself wondering why in the world she hadn't taken the guitar out of the closet back in September.

As it had since she started playing at the age of eight, the guitar relaxed her, made her feel alive, gave her confidence that was real instead of contrived. Soon, she was treating the old Martin like the dear friend and companion that it had always been, and sharing that friend with other, listening friends.

But not Chris. Not yet. She was still warming up to the idea of springing the truth on him about being a musician. Surprisingly, she found herself enjoying his company as a friend —and frequently.

Together, they had good, quiet talks between his performance sets at The Cup. Occasionally they had lunch together at the SUB. And with increasing frequency, they went for walks around the U-District—once even spontaneously stopping to see an old movie in one of the cool old theaters that dotted the funky District.

Kenzie was amazed to discover that a computer science major, albeit a musical one, had a taste for old movies. That night, the theater was having an Elvis festival. Kenzie had to bite her tongue to keep from telling Chris all about her dad, his travels with Elvis, and the smokin', rockabilly guitar riffs of her father's that could be heard on any oldies station on any given day.

Soon enough, she thought. *We need to get to know other things first. He might be intimidated by all that.*

Compared to her first term at PCU, and especially compared to the stressful first half of the current semester, Kenzie was blissfully calm in her new easy-going relationships with her suite-mates and other friends. Gradually, she knew she'd reveal the musical side of herself to the Young Life crew and to Chris. She wondered if he'd be going to Malibu this summer—Drew and Allie and some others had been talking about applying to work on the summer staff with other college students from the West Coast.

It might be fun to play music up there, during summer staff worship nights…Hmm.

But there were still weeks to make decisions about summer. Before that, she'd have exams to take, papers to write, and all kinds of fun to have. Especially her "birthday-slash-Valentine's Day," as Allie called it, and the "Heartbreak Hotel" party. *What a blast. Wish Chris could be there for it. Too bad he has to work that night.*

February 14 was unusually warm and sunny, a gift, Kenzie thought—not just for her birthday, but for all the young love blooming on the PCU campus. *I'm not sure I'm in that category yet with Chris, but I'm not in a hurry.*

Allie, on the other hand, was in a BIG hurry, all day, making preparations for the "Heartbreak Hotel" party. She'd made signs on the computer and invitations that looked like hotel guest forms. She'd also created "room service" menus, complete with hilarious tidbits about Valentine's Day losers and Kenzie's big nineteenth birthday.

Characteristically unromantic, Ryan forgot to bring flowers, but did plan to take Cooper out that night.

Emily and Kenzie had made bets on whether Beth's boyfriend would come through at all, and he did, barely, with a bunch of carnations from the grocery store. No one acknowledged their origin, despite the supermarket sticker on the paper wrapping. Kenzie secretly wondered if he was angry about Beth's newly chaste behavior, and was punishing her subtly with the cheap flowers.

As for Emily, the day was a mixed blessing. "Okay, so Mr. Cute Waiter is history. I don't care. These poetic guys are flaky."

Kenzie commiserated. "I was expecting him to show with hand-picked wildflowers and a poem—Emily Dickinson, of course. Hand-lettered on a card, and then he'd recite it in person. But it's just as well. Besides…I think he's a creep and you should dump him."

Emily laughed. Kenzie's expression was now used widely in the suite, whenever anyone of the male persuasion did anything wrong—whether he was an actual boyfriend or simply a secret crush.

"Yep, I think you're right. I'll dump him…if he ever calls. This way, I can go to the 'Heartbreak Hotel' party, as a legitimate loser."

Just then, there was a knock on the door of the suite. Opening the door, Kenzie found a green-uniformed delivery man, bearing a huge floral arrangement. The flowers came from the most expensive florist in town, according to Emily, who somehow knew such things. It was a gorgeous bouquet, with a card that read, "To our dear Valentine baby, Mary Mackenzie—Happy Birthday, Honey. There's a surprise coming—All Our Love, Mom and Dad."

Kenzie got misty, reading the card, and pinned it to the bulletin board in the suite living room. "They're the best. I wish they could be here. I've never had a birthday away from home, that I can remember."

"I wonder what the surprise is?" wondered Ryan, who had popped in. "New car? New couch? Now that would be a present. One to share with your friends."

Kenzie shook her head. "Beats me. You never know with them. Probably luggage. That's a nineteenth birthday kind of present. Hey, speaking of birthdays, kids—we've got a party to get ready for!"

The late afternoon and evening of Kenzie's birthday were crammed full of last-minute details for the Elvis and Priscilla caper. Allie went to the trouble of getting her hair "bouffed" up at a salon, "high enough to nest birds in it," Ethan said later.

Drew showed up with a motorcycle and leather jacket, looking like a pretty decent Elvis, duck-tailed hair and all. With her beehive hair, fishnet hose, miniskirt and the too-big white go-go boots, "Priscilla" climbed on the back of "Elvis's" motorcycle, and they headed for Young Life Leadership at the Garretts' with a carful of friends in tow.

At the Garretts' house near U-Dub, Drew pulled his bike right up to the front door, revved the motor loud enough for all to hear, and got off the bike with a cool attitude befitting the King of Rock and Roll. Taking Allie's arm, he strode confidently into the house, as if they were the main attraction. Inside, Drew played air guitar on "Hound Dog," followed by

"Don't Be Cruel," and "Heartbreak Hotel," which brought the house down as Drew hopped up on the fireplace, grabbed an imaginary microphone, and swung his hips like the King himself.

At the end of the song, he said in a halfway-decent Elvis voice, "Thank you very much…" and left with Allie on his arm. "Elvis has left the building," said Hank, one of the Young Life staff guys, in a deep, concert-announcer voice.

It was a great moment, a triumph, and Kenzie reveled in it.

Afterward, back at the suite, Elvis CDs were played, pizza was devoured, and "The Losers" did the Twist, the Jerk, and all the old 1960s dances they'd seen their parents do. After eating hunks of the specially decorated "Heartbreak Hotel" cake, topped with Kenzie's favorite ice cream, the gang headed for The Cup and Chaucer to catch Chris's last set, at the request of the birthday girl.

Chris was in a fine mood, as playful as Kenzie had ever seen him. No reflective, intensely personal songs tonight—he cranked up all the moldy-oldie requests the gang could throw at him, and then some.

"More Elvis!" yelled Drew, who was totally into his role as The King.

Chris obliged. When Kenzie yelled for the Beach Boys, Chris plugged in his 1965 Fender Telecaster and lit into the Chuck Berryesque riff that started "Surfin' USA," which made Kenzie go crazy with envy.

But it was Emily's request for the Beatles that made Chris the happiest—they and Phil Keaggy had been the biggest musical influences in Chris's own songwriting. He played at least ten Beatles songs that night, and while Kenzie laughed and danced with Drew, Ryan, and even shy Ethan, she found herself wishing she had spilled the beans to Chris about her own passion for playing. *I could be playing with him right now. What a blast that would be.*

Two lattés into the evening, Allie disappeared without a warning, still wearing the beehive hairdo. Fifteen minutes later, The Cup's front door opened with a slam, and Allie reappeared, with Johnny and Peggy Dawson in tow.

"SURPRISE!!!" The whole gang of friends yelled in unison with Kenzie's folks, who rushed to engulf Kenzie in a tearful double hug.

"We couldn't have missed this! It's your last teenager birthday!" explained Kenzie's mom, a tall, slender, still-athletic beauty who could beat any of her daughters on the tennis court.

"I know I just saw you," Kenzie's dad said. "But I had to come anyway, and bring your mom. She was jealous that I got to spend some time with you. And she reminded me that Seattle would make a nice Valentine's weekend getaway, too. You girls and your romantic fantasies!" He flashed that smile, hugged his "favorite" daughter again, and all was well with Kenzie's world.

"Well, introductions, Birthday Girl! We want to meet these famous friends of yours!"

"They're not all here, y'all. A lot of 'em had dates."

Allie adjusted her beehive hairdo and jumped up from her chair.

"Oh, that's what YOU think!" She dashed to the front door and, within two minutes, came back with Ryan, Cooper, and even Beth and Brad in tow.

"HAPPY BIRTHDAY!" The chorus of good wishes, combined with the emotion of the surprise visit, made Kenzie's eyes well up with tears.

"Honey, are you crying? Oh, sweetheart…" Kenzie's mom folded her youngest daughter in a warm embrace, and the tears flowed freely for a moment.

Kenzie pulled away and looked at her friends. "My nose...I need a napkin...Allie, can you..."

But she didn't even care. She didn't care that her mascara was running, that her nose was dripping (until Mom came to the rescue with a tissue), or that every dear friend she had at PCU was watching the normally cool Kenzie lose her cool. She even smiled at Chris through her messy tears, happy that she didn't worry what he'd think.

Mom and Dad were here. Her friends were here. Life at PCU was different, forever changed. A new comfort and confidence could take her safely through the next three years. And there were lattés to be consumed.

"Dad? There are some people here who have spent a lot of hard-earned dough on LightSong CDs. I figure you owe 'em. Lattés are on you!"

Johnny Dawson laughed and walked up to the coffee bar, where Maddy McDonald stood at the ready, amused, watching the whole scene.

"Better fire up that fancy espresso machine, gal. This is a drinkin' crew, I can tell. And we've got some music here, don't we? When is this Chris fella going to get rockin'?"

For the third time, Allie jumped up and ran. This time, to behind the counter, where she pulled out a familiar black guitar case—Kenzie's Martin.

"Okay, Birthday Girl—time for you to sing for your latté. How 'bout you and the old man doing a little duet? Show us how it's done down in Nashville."

Kenzie froze for a minute. *Uh-oh. The moment of truth. Here goes.*

"You mean instead of how it's done in the airport?" Kenzie grinned and accepted the guitar that Allie had unpacked.

Settling onto the edge of an overstuffed chair, she cradled the Martin in her arms and pulled a flat pick from the pocket of her jeans—carrying picks was a habit she'd returned to of late.

"Dad? How 'bout it? I'll bet Chris would let you use one of his guitars."

Chris looked stunned, but quickly responded by offering his Telecaster to Mr. Dawson. Cooper and Ryan stood up and gave Kenzie's dad their spot on the couch, and within two minutes Johnny and his daughter were tuned and ready to jam.

"What'll it be, Keeks? Carter Family? How 'bout pickin' the 'Wildwood Flower?' You know how Mr. Acuff loved that."

Kenzie smiled and glanced at her friends: Ethan, Drew, Cooper, Ryan, Beth, Brad, Emily, Allie and Chris. She touched her dad's arm, poised and ready for a song.

"Do y'all know that my dad used to play at the Grand Ole Opry?" Pride was radiating from her face.

"What's the Grand Ole Opry?" Drew asked. Kenzie and her parents burst out laughing.

"Well, that'll keep you humble!" said Mr. Dawson. "Son, it's an old-fashioned thing. Not exactly your speed, I'm sure. But you've heard of Minnie Pearl, right? Well, never mind—" He smiled to let Drew know that it was all right.

"And…" Kenzie beamed. "Dad used to play in Elvis's band. Matter of fact, you know those Elvis oldies? Dad played all the cool guitar parts. Now that's hip, don'tcha think?"

"Wow…"

"Cool…"

"Elvis? That's so awesome!"

That one impressed the gang.

"What'll it be, Dad? Elvis or the Opry?" Kenzie held her Martin at the ready, pick lightly grasped between the thumb and first finger of her right hand.

Chris perked up from his post on the chair, where he'd moved to be closer to Kenzie. "How about 'Don't Be Cruel'? I'd like to hear that— " He blushed. "If Kenzie knows it, that is—"

"Two, three, four…" Johnny Dawson swung into a country-sounding rendition of the Elvis hit. Kenzie joined right in, like she'd been doing it all her life, chiming in with harmonies to the creaky vocal lead of her dad, whose musical gifts were purely instrumental. When it came time for the guitar solo, Kenzie's dad nodded to her, and she took the lead, much to the amazement of her friends, her parents, and especially Chris, who sat on the edge of his chair, his mouth hanging open.

"Whoa…" As the song ended, the room exploded into cheers and wild applause, even from The Cup patrons who thought they'd stumbled onto a new entertainment find. Chris looked at Kenzie in a daze.

Kenzie leaned over her guitar, and accepted a spontaneous hug from him, smiling at her mom from behind Chris's shoulder.

"I…I…I had no idea," Chris stammered. "Why didn't you tell me? You're incredible! You should be playing here, not me! Or with me, maybe."

"Well, maybe I just will. As you can see, Chris," Kenzie turned to her dad and winked, " it kinda runs in the family."

N U M B E R 1
FRESHMAN BLUES

By Wendy Lee Nentwig
ISBN 0-88070-947-2

Emily Stewart has looked forward to her freshman year at PCU for years. But things don't go quite as planned. When Emily's best friend loses her financial aid, Emily finds herself rooming instead with a sloppy New Yorker named Cooper. Not only that, but Em has to deal with her over-protective brother (who decides to date Cooper!), peer pressure, new friends, and college deadlines...not to mention inedible dorm food.

Further complications arise when Emily meets what may be the man of her dreams. At first, John Wehmeyer seems to be exactly the type of guy she has been waiting for: gorgeous, romantic, and a Christian! Best of all, John thinks that Emily is wonderful, too. But when conflicts arise, Emily learns the hard way that true love is about more than romance.

Yet, even as a frightening and climactic confrontation leaves her stranded far from campus, Emily makes exciting discoveries about herself and rediscovers an incredible source of strength that will see her through her *Freshman Blues* and beyond.

N U M B E R 2
HOMEWARD HEART

By Lissa Halls Johnson
ISBN 0-88070-948-0

Maddy MacDonald's first year at PCU brings yet another new beginning for the girl who spent her childhood moving from town to town. This time, however, quirky Maddy has made up her mind to set down roots. Unfortunately, that's easier said than done after she finds herself in all kinds of trouble—trouble that threatens her future at PCU.

As it turns out, Maddy's fun-loving boyfriend, Kick, may love fun just a little too much—and he seems determined to get Maddy to join him in his adventures. Yet, even as Maddy strives to avoid the party scene, her mere association with Kick may provide exactly the ammunition a disgruntled coworker needs to get her booted out of the library—and the school—for good.

Will an unfortunate misunderstanding lead to her dismissal from the college? Or will Maddy finally find an anchor for her *Homeward Heart*?

Available at your local Christian bookstore.
If it is not in stock, ask them to special order it for you!

N U M **4** B E R
SPRING BREAK

By Wendy Lee Nentwig
ISBN 0-88070-950-2

Cooper Ellis's life is just beginning to come together. Looking for something different, the ex-professional model has left her home in New York City for college in the beautiful Pacific Northwest.

At school in Seattle she gets a great roommate and snags the guy of her dreams, a starting guard on PCU's basketball team. But after six perfect months together, her boyfriend starts having doubts about their relationship and Cooper's spring break plans are turned upside-down. And it doesn't help matters that just when her relationship is on the rocks, everyone around her seems to be pairing up.

Forced to spend spring break far from her PCU friends, Cooper has a lot of time to rethink her relationships, her decision to attend PCU, and her place in the great, big world. But as she struggles with those questions, God shows Cooper that in order to see his plan she didn't need to go all the way to Seattle...she just had to open her eyes.

Available after September 1996 at your local Christian bookstore.
If it is not in stock, ask them to special order it for you!